AVID XPRESS PRO AND DV
ON THE SPOT

AVID XPRESS PRO & DV

ON THE SPOT

TIME-SAVING TIPS & SHORTCUTS
FROM THE PROS

by Steve Hullfish

Christopher Phrommayon

Bob Donlon

DV Digital Video
EXPERT SERIES

CMP Books
San Francisco, CA

Published by CMP Books
an imprint of CMP Media LLC
Main office: 600 Harrison Street, San Francisco, CA 94107 USA
Tel: 415-947-6615; Fax: 415-947-6015
Editorial office: 4601 West 6th St, Suite B, Lawrence, KS 66049 USA
www.cmpbooks.com
email: books@cmp.com

Designations used by companies to distinguish their products are often claimed as trademarks. In all instances where CMP is aware of a trademark claim, the product name appears in initial capital letters, in all capital letters, or in accordance with the vendor's capitalization preference. Readers should contact the appropriate companies for more complete information on trademarks and trademark registrations. All trademarks and registered trademarks in this book are the property of their respective holders.

The publisher does not offer any warranties and does not guarantee the accuracy, adequacy, or completeness of any information herein and is not responsible for any errors or omissions. The publisher assumes no liability for damages resulting from the use of the information in this book or for any infringement of the intellectual property rights of third parties that would result from the use of this information.

Series Editor	Richard Harrington
Managing Editor	Gail Saari
Cover Design:	Damien Castaneda

Distributed to the book trade in the U.S. by:
Publishers Group West
1700 Fourth Street
Berkeley, CA 94710
1-800-788-3123

Distributed in Canada by:
Jaguar Book Group
100 Armstrong Avenue
Georgetown, Ontario M6K 3E7 Canada
905-877-4483

For individual orders and for information on special discounts for quantity orders, please contact:
CMP Books Distribution Center, 6600 Silacci Way, Gilroy, CA 95020
Tel: 1-800-500-6875 or 408-848-3854; Fax: 408-848-5784
email: cmp@rushorder.com; Web: www.cmpbooks.com

04 05 06 07 08   5 4 3 2 1

ISBN: 1-57820-254-X

Dedication

This book is dedicated to my family.

>   – Christopher Phrommayon

To my mom and dad, who instilled in me the importance of writing and creativity, and my wife, Jody, and children, Haley and Quinn, who lost a lot of quality time so that I could get this finished. Without their patience and understanding, this book never could have been completed.

>   – Steve Hullfish

For Anne-Lise.

>   – Bob Donlon

Contents

The first step is being able to master the interface and getting it to work for you as fast as possible. Workspaces, interface adjustments and interface tricks are covered here.

Each system can be customized by adjusting buttons and settings to help you work faster. But knowing what to adjust is critical!

A large percentage of your work is performed in the Timeline. It serves as the primary tool for interacting with your virtual film or videotape. Learning how to master all of its features will help to make your job a lot easier.

Most creative people are messy people. Not only is cleanliness next to godliness, but it will make you more efficient as well. So get yourself "organazized." It will help you to think straight.

The faster footage is recorded, the sooner you're editing. All the tricks of fast recording and batch-recording are unlocked here. Hours and hours can be saved instead of grabbing each shot by shot. Importing can be hell. Learning the right clues about your imports can prevent headaches when bringing in stills and movie files (QuickTime, Avid).

Keeping it legal, creating moods, and fixing color balance can save footage, save a show, and make a shot that doesn't work, *work*.

Whether you've been using Avid for 15 days or 15 years, you'll always find newer, faster, and better ways of doing things. In the time-sensitive world of postproduction, every second counts. These tips will help you conserve those precious minutes, hours, and possibly days to meet those tight deadlines.

8 A Cut Above 118

Transition effects are more than just dissolves, wipes, and page peels. This chapter will teach you several tricks for building custom transition effects. Whether you are editing weddings, corporate videos, children's programming, or DVD menus, learn how to spice it up to be a cut above the rest.

9 Notching It Up 130

Taking your effects to the next level and beyond. Effects can be deep on Avid products ... see the most efficient ways to pump your effects up so you can use them over and over again.

10 Text Is Your Friend 148

If the pen is mightier than the sword, then the Title Tool puts an entire armory at your disposal. People who criticize the Title Tool don't realize its full potential. Quit complaining, and read this chapter!

11 What Was That? 168

Audio is half the picture. Fixing that audio is what will make it sound right. Mixing tricks, removing hums, making it all sound right.

12 Digitally Outstanding 196

Your client is going to need stills for print as well as files for the Web and for DVD. Don't just make them once ... make it easy to make them over and over and over again.

13 Media Management 214

When the show is over, it's not over. Clients ask for redesigns weeks, months, and even years later. It's important to know what to back up, how to back it up, and how to do so quickly, even in case of a catastrophic loss. Only the essential tips, quick and fast here.

14 Troubleshooting 236

What if you could find all the tips you needed for basic video troubleshooting all in one place? What if the most common tips and preventative maintenance were available at your fingertips? Now they are.

Introduction

What's On the Spot All About?

It's getting tough to get ahead these days. Editors are expected to know so many things… from graphics to audio, DVD authoring to Web compression. The truth of the matter is it's getting hard to keep up with technology. On top of it all, professionals are getting too busy (and too competitive) to share knowledge. That's where we come in.

The On the Spot series was created to help those who want to notch their skills up. Our approach is to pair you with top industry professionals and certified instructors who are willing to share their knowledge. These generous pros are willing to share their secrets for getting the job done.

Why You Need this Book.

Simply put, mastering Avid is tough. I know firsthand. It was the first edit system I learned. I remember reading the manual as well as hovering over other editors' shoulders and watching them. I've had the fortune to participate in Avid's Master Editor Workshop as well as their certified instructor program. Despite all of this training and ten years of hands-on experience, I learned new things in this book. The Avid software is DEEP! If you are honest that you can't possibly know it all, then you can become a better editor.

Who Is This Book For?

If you read the back of the book, you've seen that we've targeted this series towards Intermediate-Advanced users. But since you work in a creative field, you probably don't follow rules very well. The truth is, anyone can read this book and get something from it… but let's set a few things straight.

A beginner can read any book, and get something from it… but you may have to work harder. Don't be afraid of being labeled a beginner; it just means you're starting out on an exciting new journey. We've all been there, and even pros will often try and pick up a new skill (and start all over again).

But hey, you're probably an intermediate user. In fact 95% of folks consider themselves intermediates (okay I made that up, but it's based on unscientific surveys at training conferences). The truth is, way too many people consider themselves to be intermediate users. There is no official time requirement you see, but sheer experience and knowledge is the real test. We've written this book to jump-start your technique. Reading alone won't make you a pro, but the knowledge in this book comes from over thirty years of hands-on experience. If you are open to learning new things (as well as unlearning some bad habits) you can definitely become a better editor.

And for you pros, you are wise enough to know that a few nuggets of wisdom are always worth a search. Depending on your experience level, you may know some of these tips (but hey, it's not a contest). Focus on what you need to know… when you find a new trick or technique; the time-savings alone will quickly pay for the book and your effort to read it.

How to Get the Most from This Book

Don't try to read the book linearly. Shop for ideas, jump around a lot, and work your way through the chapters you need most. We've left extra space by the tips so you can jot down your own notes. If you're a mobile editor, this book should fit nicely in your bag. Hit a tough spot, and just pull the book out when the client leaves the room to check for a new idea or a troubleshooting tip. Have a few minutes to kill, read a tip. We bet you'll return to the application with some new ideas and new energy.

Is This Everything?

Of course not… but it is the most essential information and coolest tricks we thought you needed to know. There are plenty of great classes, online resources, and conferences worth checking out. And speaking as someone who's often been told to RTFM (Read the ____ Manual) I can assure you that there's good stuff in there too. We've just put the best stuff at your fingertips. Dig in, start to learn, and share this knowledge with others. Have fun… and remember, "The power is in the trim."

Richard Harrington

June 2004

Series Creator and Editor

 Tips marked with the Pro Special icon are written for Avid Xpress Pro users.

ON THE SPOT

CHAPTER 1

Interface Tricks

The interface is where you live and breathe. The goal of the interface is to allow you to effortlessly manipulate your footage. There are many hidden secrets of the Avid interface that can help you achieve that kind of "Vulcan mind meld" that can take you to the next level of editing. The interface holds not only the key to editing faster but also to editing more artfully and with greater craftsmanship.

Avid is known for a great user interface, so this chapter—and this whole book—is dedicated to exploiting all of the great stuff that helps get your ideas from your brain, through your fingers, and onto the screen with the least amount of effort.

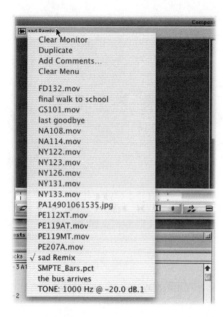

Look Ma, No Bins!

Once you've called a clip into the source window, even if you didn't edit from it, you can call that clip back without finding it again in a bin.

The source monitor menu, which is above the source monitor, includes the last 20 clips that have been called into the monitor.

- Click on the source monitor menu and select the clip you want from the alphabetical list.

- To display the most recently loaded clip at the top of the list, Alt+click (Opt+click) the source monitor menu.

Screen Real Estate

Don't forget the rest of the GUI when mapping buttons. While the keyboard is an attractive place to remap buttons, the onscreen buttons should be looked at as well. The onscreen buttons are perfect for two kinds of shortcuts: those that you rarely use, so you need to see them, and those that are used in conjunction with mouse movement anyway. For example, it's almost impossible to set up a Collapse without using the mouse, so while you're mousing anyway, you might as well just click up above the Timeline to execute that command instead of keyboarding it.

Look Ma, No Monitors!

You should really be editing while looking at a video monitor. And if you are, it makes the monitors in the Composer Window kind of superfluous. What you *do* need are the Timelines.

- To minimize the Composer Window to just the Timelines and buttons, you can click on the bottom-right corner of the monitor so that the cursor turns into a small rectangular box and drag upwards, and the monitors will disappear.

- To eliminate all the dragging, you can also right-click on the Composer Monitor and choose Hide Monitors from the contextual menu (PC) or click on the zoom button in the top-right corner (Mac).

While the monitors are hidden, you can still load video into the Timelines and edit as you would normally.

Cache Money!

If one of the monitors in the Composer Window is active and you type a timecode number using the numeric keypad (no need to use colons or semicolons), the Timeline locator will jump to that timecode. Typing a timecode number preceded by a "+" will jump forward in the Timeline by that amount, and typing a "-" will jump backwards.

The timesaving tip here is that the computer stores this number in a cache, so if you want to leap forward by the same amount over and over, you don't have to type the number again and again. Just press Enter, and the last number pad entry is called up from the cache.

Would You Like a Bigger Timeline Track?

With limited screen real estate, it really does pay to have customized Timeline views: some with larger audio tracks for viewing auto gain or sample plots and others with a maximum number of tracks in a minimum amount of space for complex projects.

You can click and drag on the line between tracks in the track panel to change size.

But since we're always crusading for greater use of the keyboard, we'd recommend:

- Select the tracks you want to resize in the track panel

- Press Ctrl+L (Command+L) to enLarge.

- Press Ctrl+K (Command+K) to shrinK.

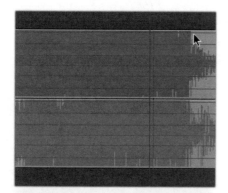

Preparation K: How to Shrink Your ... Sample Plots

Often, when you import CD audio and try to view the sample plots in the Timeline, the sample plots are so large that you can't see the peaks. They're off the scale! You can resize the audio sample plots within the Timeline audio tracks in much the same way that you resize the tracks themselves.

- Select the tracks you want to resize in the track panel.

- Press Ctrl+Alt+L (Cmd+Opt+L) to enLarge.

- Press Ctrl+Alt+K (Cmd+Opt+K) to shrinK.

The two screenshots are "before and "after" from the same section of the Timeline.

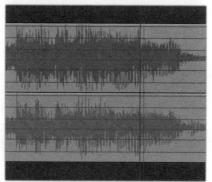

Stop the Samples!

If you like to view your audio sample plots in the Timeline but accidentally open a huge project with them active, you'll wait forever for the Timeline to redraw. You can stop a screen redraw the same way you stop almost any other computer function: Ctrl+. (Command+.).

This allows you to either turn off sample plots in the Timeline fast menu or, in your Timeline settings, choose Show Marked Waveforms.

With Show Marked Waveforms chosen in your Timeline settings, you only see the waveforms–or Samples–in between your Mark In and Mark Out.

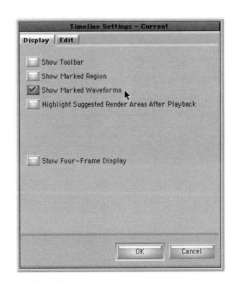

Stack 'Em Up

Adding tracks using keyboard commands is convenient and simple.

- Press Ctrl+Y (Command+Y) for a new video track.

- Press Ctrl+U (Command+U) for a new audio track.

You can also add tracks out of sequence, so you can have v1 then v3 then v5.

- Pressing Ctrl+Alt+Y (Cmd+Opt+Y) or Ctrl+Alt+U (Cmd+Opt+U) will call up the Add Track Dialog box.

- Using the Add Track dialog box, you can specify what kind of track (audio, video or even Meta track) and what track number you'd like to create.

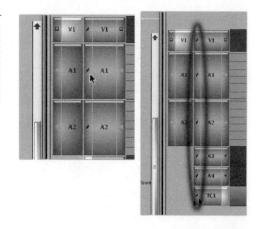

In Sync

One of the ways you can make sure that your lip sync doesn't get knocked off from trimming or splice edits is by turning on Sync Lock.

- To enable Sync Lock on a single track, click on the area between the source and sequence tracks in the track panel. A small slash should appear, indicating that Sync Lock is on.

- To enable Sync Lock on all tracks, which is probably a more common thing to do, click on the area between the source and sequence tracks in the track panel's timecode track. Clicking on it again will toggle Sync Lock off for all tracks.

Pick a Track, Any Track

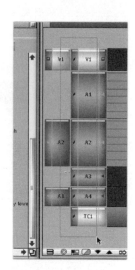

Knowing all of the ways to select tracks can save time.

- Keyboard selection (using the default keyboard setup) is easy. Press the assigned keyboard numbers (See figure 8.1.) on the QWERTY keyboard: 7, 8, 9, 0, - and =. These work as toggles, so if the track is selected, pressing the corresponding button will deselect the track.

- Press Ctrl+A (Command+A) to select all of the tracks.

- Press Shift+Ctrl+A (Shift+Command+A) to de-select all of the tracks.

- Lasso the tracks in the track panel to invert the selection—turning enabled tracks to disabled tracks and vice versa.

Sometimes these methods are best used in concert. For example, if you've got several tracks selected and you just want v1, use the keyboard shortcut to deselect all tracks, then press 8. Or if you want everything except v1, select all tracks and then press 8.

Lock Down!

When you've got a final sequence and you want to make sure that no one—including you, by mistake—changes the sequence, you can lock one track or all of them.

- Select the tracks you want to lock and choose Lock Tracks from the Clip Menu.

This adds tiny padlock icons to the tracks in the track panel, and any attempt to edit or trim these tracks result in the warning: "Cannot edit a read-only track."

- To edit these tracks again, select the tracks to unlock and choose Unlock Tracks from the Clip Menu.

Head Lock in Segment Mode

When dragging clips in the Timeline using Segment Mode, you can drag and drop the clip at any point, or you can use modifier keys to either lock the head of the clip to the tail of another clip or lock the tail of the clip to the head of another clip, which is similar to back-timing a clip.

- Choose one of the two Segment Modes, either with the keyboard (semi-colon and apostrophe keys) or with the red and yellow arrows at the bottom-left corner of the Timeline.

- Hold down Ctrl (Command) while dragging the segment to lock it to headframes. This is the default method used in Xpress DV.

- Hold down Ctrl+Alt (Cmd+Opt) while dragging the segment to lock to tailframes.

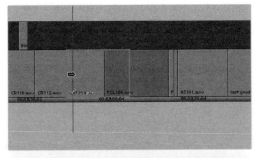
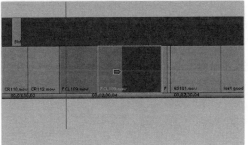

Zoom!

There are multiple methods of zooming in the Timeline. Zooming into the Timeline helps to make precise Timeline edits and to examine sections of the Timeline in greater detail.

- Drag the Scale Bar, which is just to the right of the Timeline View menu. Dragging to the right zooms in and to the left zooms out.

- The three keyboard shortcuts most commonly used for Timeline zooming are:

  - Ctrl+[(Command+[) to zoom out

  - Ctrl+] (Command+]) to zoom in

  - Ctrl+/ (Command+/) to view the entire Timeline

- For precise custom zooms to specific locations not centered on the current Timeline position, Ctrl+M (Command+M) allows you to lasso a specific area of the Timeline and zoom into that region. Ctrl+J (Command+J) zooms out.

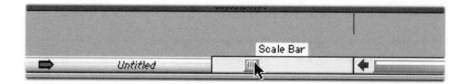

No Way Out

While workspaces are great, there is no Return to Normal button to get you out of a workspace. If this is something you feel you need, then you can create a basic or blank workspace to get you back to regular editing. Consider mapping this workspace to a key for a quick changeover.

Mark Your SpoT

A very common method for marking ins and outs is to use segment boundaries that already exist. The tool for doing this is called Mark Clip.

- Place the Timeline locator (the vertical blue line in the Timeline) within the bounds of the clip you want to mark and select the track that corresponds to the segment you want to mark.

- Press the T key if you're using the default keyboard layout. This places a Mark In at the head of the clip and a Mark Out at the tail. Or click on the Mark Clip button at the top of the Timeline toolbar or under the sequence monitor.

- If you'd like to mark a clip but don't want to have it use the selected tracks, Alt+click (Opt+click) on the Mark Clip button or key. This seeks out the closest Mark In and the closest Mark Out to the current Timeline location.

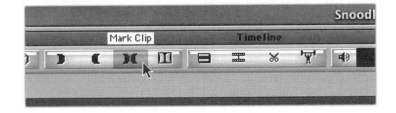

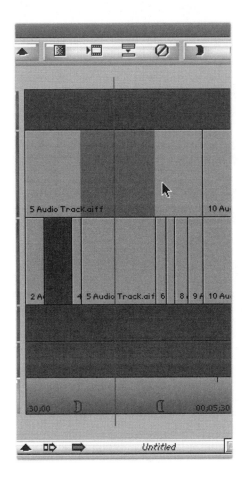

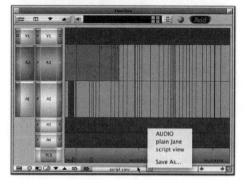

Find the Script Page in the Timeline

A common request from a producer would be, "let's kill the third soundbite on page six." But your Timeline doesn't have page numbers so that doesn't do you much good. Well, how'd you like to add page numbers to the Timeline?

❶ When you are done with your rough edit, use the segment arrows to select all of the soundbites and clips on the first page of the script. You need to do this on only one of your audio tracks.

❷ Go to the Sequence Monitor menu (click on the name of the sequence above the Sequence Monitor), and choose Add Comments.

❸ In the Comments Window, type "1" and click OK.

❹ In the Timeline Fast Menu, uncheck Clip Names or any other text choices and check Clip Comments. Save this Timeline view.

❺ Now, in your Timeline, all of the selected clips have a "1" in them. Repeat steps 1–3 for each page of the script. This will go a lot faster if you map the Add Comments menu selection to a keystroke. You should be able to do an entire 30-page script in under two minutes. Think of the time you'll save!

Where Did Center Duration Go?

Many Avid users who move to Xpress Pro or DV from higher level models will miss Center Duration in their Composer window. Center Duration shows the duration between a Mark In and a Mark Out in the Composer window between the source and the Sequence monitor, hence "Center Duration." To replace this important item, you can create a "fake" duration counter by calling up the timecode window from the Tools menu and setting it to IO, then shrinking it and placing it near the Composer window. Be sure to save this setup using either a toolset or a workspace.

A Faster Redraw

To get better performance, create a Timeline view with almost no information. This improves screen redraw times and doesn't tax the system resources as heavily. You should definitely turn off Clip Frames, and don't use the Film track in Show Tracks. See if you can edit with no text in the Timeline. Once you've created this Timeline, save it with a descriptive name using the View Menu at the bottom of the Timeline. This one is called "Fast Redraw." Are you tough enough to edit without Clip Names?

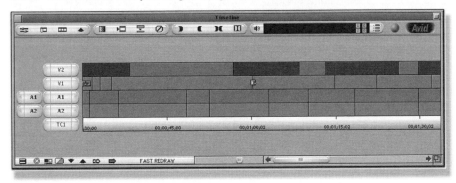

Outstanding in Your Field

When you use the arrow buttons to step through a transition frame by frame, you are seeing only the first field of the frame. So, if you are cutting pre-edited material, or close to camera edits, you can miss flash fields. To see flash fields and other things, like tape hits that exist only on field 2, there are "Step Forward One Field" and "Step Backward One Field" buttons. You can access them from the Command Palette (Ctrl+3 (Command I 3)) in the Move tab. Map them to your keyboard. We have them at Shift-Left arrow and Shift-Right arrow.

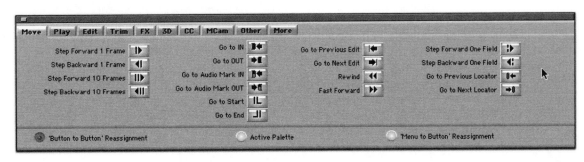

ON THE SPOT

Make the System Yours

It is very easy when you first start to learn the Avid interface to edit so fast that you never bother with all of the stuff that doesn't really "edit." This is one reason why so many people miss out on the inherent power that they can gain by customizing Xpress Pro.

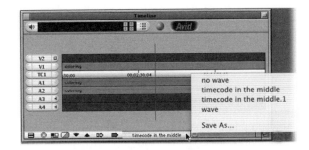

Customizing your interface is crucial in the Avid environment, which is designed to accommodate many different editors working on many different kinds of projects. Instead of using Xpress Pro or DV the way it's designed for the masses, make it work *for* you by redesigning it to your unique style and workflow. Customizing the interface to the way *you* work leverages every click of every button.

KISS – Keep It Simple for Settings

When you are searching through settings, it helps to have a nice, streamlined list to search through. The way to clean up the Settings List is with the Fast Menu in the Settings tab of the Project window. The main choices are Active Settings, All Settings, and Base Settings. There are also seven other specialized settings. Active Settings is a good one to use for general purposes. Obviously, if you choose this, you won't have access to any settings that aren't active. Base Settings is another good choice. Base settings shows all of the Project, User, and Site Settings but filters out all of the views.

Whatever Lola Fonts

What's the point of carefully naming and organizing your clips, sequences, folders, and bins if their names are too small to read? Or, perhaps your producer or client is having difficulty reading your computer screen from a distance. With the Project, Composer, Timeline, or Bin window active, choose Edit>Set Font to change or resize the text in those windows.

- Timeline fonts are saved with Timeline views, but bin fonts are not saved with bin views.

- When setting a bin font, any bins you create afterwards will also have that same font.

- Project window fonts are saved with that specific project.

- Composer window fonts are saved with the user profile.

Free Feature Upgrade!

You can add additional functionality by attempting to import settings and views from more expensive Avid models. A great example of this is that neither Xpress Pro nor Xpress DV allow you to drag Timeline tracks to new locations, enabling you to place your timecode track between your video and audio tracks in the Timeline, for example. This creates a visual separation between the video and audio tracks *and* gives easier access to clicking on the timecode track, for things like enabling Sync Lock on all tracks or exiting modes.

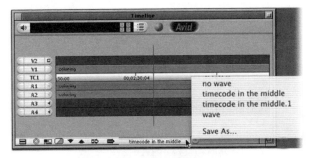

❶ On a higher-end Avid, drag the timecode track between your video and audio tracks.

❷ Save that Timeline view using the View Menu at the bottom of the Timeline.

❸ With the Settings tab open in the Project window, press Ctrl+N (Cmd+N).

❹ Drag the new Timeline view from the Settings tab to the New Settings window.

❺ Save your new setting to a removable storage device and "sneakernet" it to Xpress Pro.

❻ Call up the Settings tab of the Project window and press Ctrl+O (Cmd+O). Navigate to the location of the setting file you just copied and choose Open.

❼ Click on the words "Timeline View" in the New Settings window and drag it into the Settings List in your Project window.

❽ Call up your new Timeline view using the Timeline View menu at the bottom of the Timeline. You'll amaze other Xpress Pro users with this cool setting!

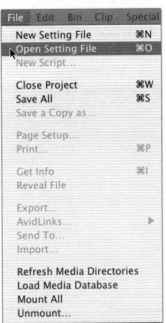

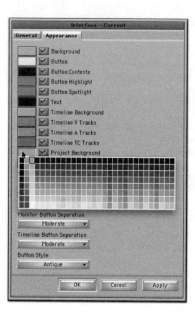

Dude, Where's My Project Window?

With multiple bins open, it's easy to lose track of which window is the Project window. Sometimes this confusion can cause you to accidentally close the project while you're quickly closing a bunch of bins. To avoid this, you can change the color of your Project window.

❶ Call up the Settings tab of your Project window.

❷ Double-click the Interface Setting with a checkmark next to it. This is your active Interface Setting. In other words, it's the one that currently controls what your interface looks like. This calls up the Interface window.

❸ Click on the Appearance tab.

❹ Click on the small box to the left of the words "Project window" and to the left of the checkmark box. This will call up a color picker dialog. Pick a color from the choices and click Apply at the bottom of the Appearance tab to see what it will look like. If you like it, click OK.

But I Like the Pretty Colors

If you don't want the window color to be different but you like the idea of something to distinguish the Project window from the other windows in your interface, then consider changing the font or font size of your Project window.

❶ With your Project window selected, choose Edit>Set Font.

❷ In the Set Font window, choose a new font or font size and click OK.

Either of these alterations will easily help you distinguish the Project window from the rest of the interface. Or memorize its keyboard shortcut: Ctrl+9 (Cmd+9), which calls the Project window to the top.

Workspace: The Final Frontier

A workspace is a group of tools and windows arranged in a customized layout. You can create a different workspace for each editing task, like mixing audio, and call it up with the touch of a button.

❶ Click on the Workspace setting at the bottom of the Settings tab in the Project window.

❷ Press Ctrl+D (Cmd+D) to duplicate it. Now you have two workspaces.

❸ Name the workspace with a check next to it. This is your active workspace. Add a name by clicking to the left of the word "User" and typing a name when you see a text cursor. Call this one "AUDIO."

❹ Arrange tools and windows for a specific purpose, for example, opening and arranging all of the audio tools.

❺ Double-click the "AUDIO" workspace and choose "Activate Settings Linked By Name," "Manually Update this Workspace," and "Save Workspace Now."

❻ To call up the workspace with a button click, double-click the Keyboard Setting in the Settings tab and press Ctrl+3 (Cmd+3) to call up the Command Palette.

❼ From the More tab of the Command Palette, drag the W1 button to a key on the keyboard, for example, the F5 key. Close the Keyboard and Command windows. Now, pressing the F5 key will call up your AUDIO workspace.

It's good to create one workspace that has no tools. Use this workspace to "clear" other workspaces without having to close each individual tool or window.

Safely Save Settings

Saving copies of your settings outside your Avid User folder is a very good idea (there's this rumor that computers can crash). Settings often become corrupted and if you haven't saved them, they will need to be re-created from scratch. Saving them to a CD or a USB thumb drive is an excellent way to be able to move your settings from one machine to another if you are freelancing or use multiple systems. In a large editing facility, it is good to have your settings saved to a central server so that they can be accessed from all of the editing systems.

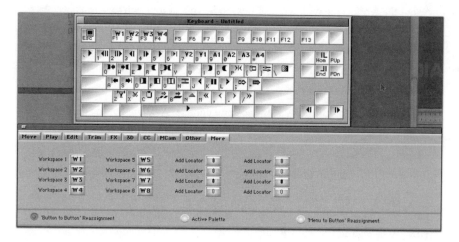

Warning

Danger A–Z

The numbering of the workspaces is based on their alphabetical order. If you'd like to use shortcut keys, call the tip "1-Audio" to force the tips into a user-specified order.

Hitting the Links with Workspaces

Workspaces were designed to call up custom groupings of tools and windows that you often use together, such as all of your audio tools. But one of the benefits of workspaces is that they can also call up links. In other words, if you click a workspace button, it will enable all of the setting and views that have the same name. You don't even have to have it organize windows; you could use workspaces just to call up settings. If you have a favorite Timeline view or bin view, naming it the same as a workspace enables that view to be called up at the touch of a button. Just choose "Activate Setting Linked By Name" in the workspace setting window.

Workspace Linking—Listen Up Now

To link a Timeline view to your AUDIO workspace:

❶ Go to the Timeline Fast Menu and click on Audio Auto Gain and Audio Sample Plot.

❷ Also, resize all of your audio tracks so that the video tracks are skinny and the audio tracks are fat. You can do this by either dragging the lines between the tracks up or down or by selecting the tracks that you wish to affect and pressing Ctrl+K (Cmd+K) to shrink the track or Ctrl+L (Cmd+L) to enlarge the track.

❸ Save the Timeline view in the Timeline View Menu at the bottom of the Timeline as AUDIO. Capitalization must be identical to your workspace name.

Now, whenever your AUDIO workspace is called up, it will also recall the AUDIO Timeline view.

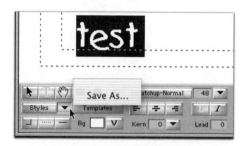

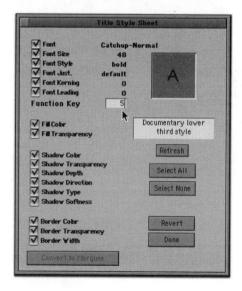

Change Title Styles with a Single Click

On many of the hardware-based character generators, you only have to click a single button to assign a new font and style for on-screen text. This is really a fast and convenient way to create titles. Believe it or not, the Avid technology can do this too!

❶ Open the Title Tool. (Choose Clip>New Title or Tools>Title Tool)

❷ Type some text and highlight it by dragging the text cursor back over it.

❸ Assign a new font and apply shadows, face colors, italics and anything else your incredibly creative and talented heart desires.

❹ Click on the Save Style Parameters button, which is the small downward-pointing triangle near the bottom of the Title Tool to the right of the word "Styles," and select the Save As option.

❺ In the Title Style Sheet window that comes up, name your style in the text box under the thumbnail image of your title style and use the numeric keypad or the numbers above the QWERTY keyboard (*not* the function keys!) to enter the number of the Function key that you would like to use to assign this style to future text. Type the number in the small text pane to the right of the words "Function Key" then save your style.

❻ Now, whenever you want to assign that style to text in the Title Tool, select it and press the function key that you assigned to the style.

Assigning styles to the function keys does not alter their function during normal editing. The function keys only assign styles while the Title Tool is open. When it is closed, the function keys continue to trigger editing commands.

Multiple Settings for Multiple Uses

You can create multiple versions of settings and switch between them with a click of the mouse. For example, you could have two trim settings: one with a very short pre-roll and another with a longer pre-roll. You could then change your pre-roll times with a single click of a button.

❶ To create two keyboard settings, call up the Settings tab of your Project window.

❷ Click on the keyboard setting. (Click on the name of the setting to select it.)

❸ Press Ctrl+D (Cmd+D) to duplicate the setting. Now you have two keyboard settings.

❹ Click to the right of the word "Keyboard" and to the left of the word "User" to name the keyboard setting.

❺ Double-click on the word "Keyboard" in the settings list and press Ctrl+3 (Cmd+3) to call up the Command Palette.

❻ Customize your keyboard and save it.

Repeat steps 4 and 5 to customize and name the other keyboard setting.

To switch between them, click in the space to the left of the word "Keyboard" in the settings list. This will place a small checkmark in that spot to indicate that the setting is active.

Producer Keyboard

Have you ever returned to the edit suite and found your producer or client standing over the keyboard? It's not a pretty sight. Create a keyboard that is all blank so that it doesn't do anything, then name it "Producer Keyboard." Enable it whenever you leave the edit suite. (The blank key is on the tab called "other" in the Command Palette.)

Menus Are for Restaurants, not Editing!

If you often mouse up to the menus at the top of the monitor to pull down a selection, you are wasting precious creative time and risking carpal tunnel syndrome. Map your most common menu pull down selections to your keyboard instead.

1 Go to the Settings tab of the Project window and choose Keyboard.

2 Press Ctrl+3 (Cmd+3) to call up the Command Palette.

3 At the bottom of the Command Palette, click on the Menu to Button Reassignment button.

4 Now, as you move your cursor over your keyboard setting window, it looks like a small pulldown menu. Click on a key of the keyboard or one of the soft buttons, like under the sequence monitor or above the Timeline.

5 Now, click on one of the menus and pull down to a selection and release the mouse. You will notice that this assigns the pull down selection to the button.

The Winner by Default!

You can have certain settings as defaults that are called up each time you create a new project or user. These custom defaults are created in your Site Settings. This is useful for things like defaulting all new projects to have 48K audio sampling rate or so that all new projects have the same default starting sequence timecode. Let's assign a starting timecode of 58:30:00 NDF to all new sequences in all new projects.

❶ Go to the Settings tab of your Project window and double-click the General setting.

❷ Type 583000 in the text box under Default Starting TC. Use a colon for non-drop frame or a semi-colon for drop frame. Click OK.

❸ Choose File>Open Settings File, or Ctrl+O (Cmd+O). Navigate to Program files>Avid>Avid Xpress Pro>Settings>Site Settings (PC) or Applications>Avid Xpress Pro>Settings>Site Settings.avs (Mac) and open the file. This calls up a small empty window called Site Settings.

❹ Drag your General setting from the Settings tab in the Project window into the Site Settings window. Close the Site Settings window.

Now, any new project will have 58:30:00 as the starting timecode. You can save any of your other user or project settings to the Site Setting window in the same manner. These changes *only* affect new users and projects created after the site setting was saved.

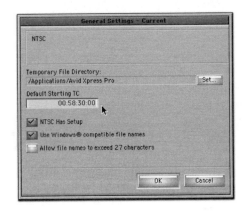

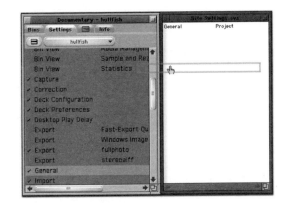

Fly "Autoconfigure Decks," FLY!

If you use the Autoconfigure Decks button in the Capture window or the Digital Cut window regularly, here's what can speed this process dramatically.

❶ On the desktop on a Mac, navigate to Applications>Avid Xpress Pro>Supporting Files>Machine Templates, and on a PC navigate to Program Files>Avid>Avid Xpress Pro>Supporting Files>Machine Templates.

❷ Open this folder and delete all the deck templates for decks you don't own— except for the ones called Generic. Or you could create a new folder called "Decks I Wish I Owned" and drag all of the deck templates for the decks you don't own in there. Now there should only be the dozen or so Generic decks plus the two or three decks that you own in the Machine_Templates folder. That got rid of more than 300 files!

Try not to blink the next time you do an Autoconfigure because "Loading deck templates" is going to flash by like lightning.

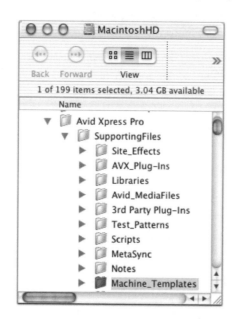
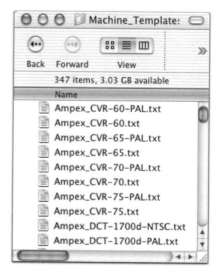

Save Yourself

Your user settings become an integral part of the way you edit, and losing them is like losing your right hand. It is fairly common for user settings to become corrupted. This shows up as strange behaviors that you may attribute to bugs in the system software. However, if you create a new user and edit with that, you often discover that the software works fine and that it must be your user settings that are corrupt.

The best way to prevent this is to save your user settings to a USB thumb drive (for easy portability to other systems) or to a CD or even a secure place somewhere on a network. Saving settings is easy and is done at the desktop level.

❶ These settings are kept in various folders on Macs and PCs depending on the version. On a Mac, they're not kept with the application in the Applications folder but usually in the Shared folder. On a PC, it's normally C:Program Files/Avid/Xpress Pro/Avid Users. If you have trouble finding the setting with your name on it, do a Find or Search for "Avid Users."

❷ Once you've located your personal user setting folder–it should be a folder with contents similar to this screenshot–copy it to the removable storage medium or another drive and you're done.

❸ If and when your user settings become corrupt, replace the corrupt version with the version you saved.

User settings can be shared between different models and versions, but this is not recommended because of the greater risk of corruption and because some features may not be compatible.

The Enforcer, Starring the Media Creation Setting!

It is so easy to import and capture media at different resolutions and to the wrong drives. If you want to clean up this problem, turn to the Media Creation setting. It should be your first stop after creating a new project.

1 Open the Media Creation setting in the Settings tab of the Project window.

2 In the Drive Filtering tab, select the drives you want to filter out.

3 In the Capture tab, select the video resolution for your project, and if you want the media to go to a specific drive, select that. We're sending our media to Big Bertha. You can automatically apply these resolutions and drive destination to any imported media, titles, or mixdowns by clicking both Apply to All buttons.

4 To apply these choices as the default on all future projects, follow the steps in the section called The Winner by Default on page 35.

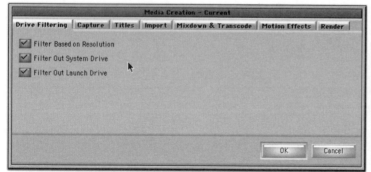

Left, Left, Left, Right, Left!

Sick of panning all of your mono media to the center on all of your audio tracks? Go to your Audio Settings in the Settings tab of the Project window and choose the All Tracks Centered button in the bottom-left corner of the window. This automatically centers the pan on all of your tracks. Our experience is that most sequences have more true mono tracks than stereo tracks. So leave this as the default, then on any true stereo tracks, like music, go into the Audio Mix Tool and pan them left and right.

Captured!

To get around 2GB file limitations, Avid created a setting within the Capture setting called "Capture to Multiple Files." This is automatically turned on and defaults to being able to save a 30-minute capture. If you want to capture longer clips in a single capture, you need to change this to whatever your longest clip is. Beware though: this feature slows down your system since the drives need to be prepared to accept this long file, so if you want better performance and you usually only capture shorter clips, you can turn off this option. When the option is turned off, the capture length is limited to the length of media that can be contained in a 2GB file size. For 1:1 media, this is quite short.

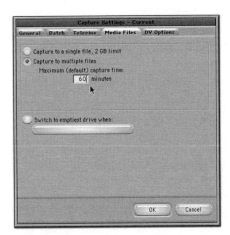

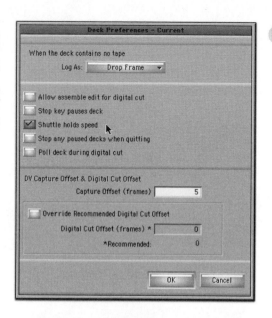

Put the Pedal to the Metal

When you are using the Capture Tool to control a deck, the default behavior for the shuttle is that you must use the mouse to hold the shuttle at a certain speed. Releasing the mouse drops the shuttle into pause. If you prefer for the shuttle speed to remain constant without holding down the mouse, the Deck Preferences setting holds the key to your happiness.

❶ Go to the Settings tab of the Project window and double-click the Deck Preferences setting.

❷ Enable "Shuttle holds speed" and click OK.

Now the tape will shuttle continuously at the speed you leave the shuttle.

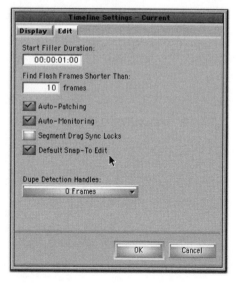

Snap!

If you are an Xpress Pro user who started out editing in Xpress DV, you may long for the days when each segment that you dragged to the Timeline automatically snapped in place to the clip before it. Avid thought there would be those who loved this feature, so they retained it by making it a setting. To get this functionality back:

❶ Go to the Settings tab of the Project window and double-click the Timeline setting.

❷ In the Edit tab of the Timeline setting window, enable "Default Snap-To-Edit" and click OK.

Now dragging clips in the Timeline automatically snaps the front of one clip to the back of the one in front of it.

Snap! The Sequel

If you like the snapping behavior caused when you enable Default To Snap but want it only occasionally, then disable it and hold down the Ctrl key while dragging segments in the Timeline (Cmd+drag on Mac) This will snap only those segments that are Ctrl+ or Cmd+dragged. That is the default behavior on most of the higher-end Avid products. You can also snap the tail frame of a clip to the head frame of a segment that is behind it by Alt+Ctrl+dragging it (Option+Cmd+dragging it).

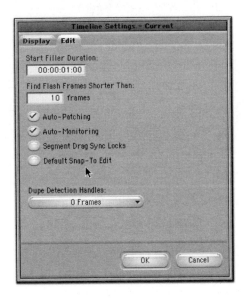

Trim Like a Pro in Pro

One of the most convenient and intuitive ways to trim in Xpress Pro is to use the J-K-L keys to play or jog the trim to where you want it, instead of using numbers.

❶ To enable J-K-L Trim, go to the Settings tab of the Project window and double-click on the Trim setting.

❷ In the Trim Settings window, select the Features tab, enable the J-K-L Trim button, then click OK.

Now, when you are in Trim Mode, you can use the JKL buttons to manipulate the trim point.

ON THE SPOT

CHAPTER 3

The Timeline Is Your Friend

A large percentage of your work is performed in the Timeline. It serves as the primary tool for interacting with your virtual film or videotape. So learning how to master all of its features will help to make your job a lot easier. How can you control the behavior of the audio sample plot? Is there a way to preview your frames in segment mode? How can you restore its default snapping behavior? Why do your track monitors change when you patch to other tracks? How can you label your segments with different colors? Can you zoom in and out of the Timeline with the keyboard? How can you mark In and Out points based on a source clip's sample plot? These questions and more will be answered in this chapter.

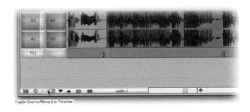

Toggle Source/Record in Timeline

Open Wide

No matter how many keyboard shortcuts you know, you may learn that the most efficient way to work is to find the right balance between the mouse and keyboard. So, if you want more space for buttons, it pays to have a computer monitor that's at least 1,280 pixels in width. If you resize your Timeline window to make it as wide as possible, you'll get more blank buttons in the Timeline toolbar, which you can map to be whichever commands your want. Unfortunately, regardless of your monitor resolution, the Timeline toolbar can hold only up to 24 buttons. If your monitor's width isn't at least 1,280 pixels, you can reveal more buttons by hiding the audio meters from the Meter Menu button.

Don't Leave Your Marked Region on Me

When you mark In and Out points in the Timeline, Avid's default behavior is to highlight that area. This is usually very useful, because you immediately know where In and Out points are set. But, what if you've got lots of clip text in your Timeline, such as Clip Duration, Clip Comments, Audio Auto Gain, or Sample Plot? Depending on your track or clip colors, you might not be able to read the text in the Timeline because the In-to-Out highlight color is in your way. So, turn it off! Go to the Settings tab in the Project window, and double-click Timeline Settings. In the Display tab of the Timeline Settings, turn off Show Marked Region, and the In-to-Out highlight is gone. You will still see the In and Out marks in the timecode track in the Timeline, so you won't be completely lost without the highlight.

Just Wave Hello

Tired of waiting for the sample plot to draw and update in the Timeline? If so, you can always interrupt it by pressing Ctrl+period (Cmd+period). Or, you can set up Avid to display the sample plot only between In and Out points.

❶ Go to the Settings tab in the Project window and double-click the Timeline Settings.

❷ In the Display tab of the Timeline Settings, turn on Show Marked Waveforms.

❸ Now, mark In and Out points in the Timeline, turn on the sample plot from the Timeline Fast Menu, and the waveforms will draw only between the In and Out points. (Note: Even the most experienced Avid editor may forget that this setting is on. So, he or she will spend hours trying to figure out why the sample plot won't show up, when it's because he or she forgot to mark In and Out points.)

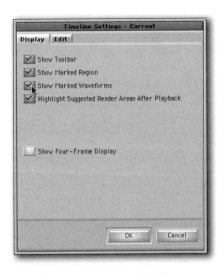

Do You Want 2 or 4?

By default, when you drag segments in Segment Mode, the Avid doesn't preview the frames that you will be changing. If you want a preview, go to the Settings tab in the Project window, and double-click the Timeline Settings. In the Display tab of the Timeline Settings, turn on Show Four-Frame Display. Although you'll be sacrificing system performance, this can help you determine where to drop segments in Segment Mode. If the Composer window is showing both the Source and Record monitors, the Avid will display the frame that will precede the dragged segment, the head and tail frames of the dragged segment, and the frame that will follow the dragged segment. If the Composer window is showing only the Record Monitor (as it is in the Basic Toolset), then the Avid will display only the preceding and following frames.

Insert Here

Normally when adding tracks, Xpress Pro goes in order. For example, if you already have A1 and A2 in your sequence, the next track to be added would be A3. But what if you have already designed assignments for the tracks and want to make an edit on A6? One option would be to continue adding tracks until A6 was reached, but this makes for an unnecessary amount of space in the Timeline. If you want to add a higher track by name, Alt+click (Opt+click) Clip>New Audio Track will present a menu where you can select the name of the new track. It's easier than managing empty tracks in your Timeline and it takes up a lot less space.

Auto-Monitoring for the People

When you patch video tracks, the Avid assumes you want to monitor the track to which you patch. If you're working with different layers of video, this default behavior may be annoying, because if you need to replace a clip in a lower track, the monitor changes so that you are no longer monitoring the entire composite. To turn off this behavior, go to the Settings tab in the Project window and double-click the Timeline Settings. In the Edit tab in the Timeline Settings, turn off Auto-Monitoring. Now, you can always monitor the topmost track while editing the tracks below.

Auto-Patching for the People

An editor is constantly patching and repatching and selecting and deselecting source and record tracks, and most often the patched and selected tracks are the same. So, save yourself a few seconds, and set up Avid for auto-patching. Go to the Settings tab in the Project window, and double-click the Timeline Settings. In the Edit tab in the Timeline Settings, turn on Auto-Patching. Now, whenever you select an audio or video record track, the corresponding source track will automatically patch to it. Speed up the processes by selecting the V1-2 and A1-4 tracks with the 7, 8, 9, 0, -, and = keys.

Do You Care to Comment?

Clip comments allow you to type text in selected segments without altering the original master clips. This is useful for leaving notes to yourself in the Timeline, such as lines or page numbers from a script, shot descriptions, instructions for effects work, or simply reminders about edit decisions.

❶ To add clip comments, enter Segment Mode and select the segment(s) for which you want to add a comment.

❷ Then, go to the Clip Name Menu above the record monitor and choose Add Comments.

❸ To see your comments in the sequence, go to the Timeline Fast Menu in the lower left corner and choose Clip Comments.

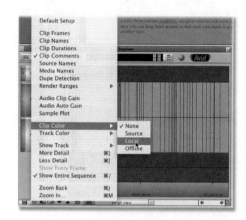

Color Your World

Another way to be able to find parts of your show with a quick glance at the Timeline is to use Local Clip Color.

❶ Go to the Timeline Fast Menu and choose Clip Color>Local. You may want to save this Timeline view so that you can call it up quickly.

❷ Select a clip or clips using the Segment Mode arrows and choose Set Local Clip Color from the Edit Menu and pick a color from the pulldown menu.

❸ Repeat these steps for any additional clips you want to identify.

You could make the opening title sequence one color and all of the commercial breaks a different color and the bumpers another color. Or make each show segment a different color.

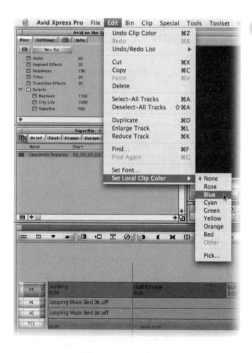

Local Color

Local clip colors allow you to tag a specific instance of a segment without affecting other instances of the same clip. This proves to be particularly useful for reference purposes. Let's say you're using archival footage and you've already got the low-quality VHS version but you don't have the DV or D1 version yet. While you wait for the high-quality tape to arrive, just edit in the low-quality clip, and tag it with a local clip color. Then, when you finally receive the high-quality footage, the local clip color will tell you exactly which clip to replace. Also, Local Clip Color can help you organize a free-form piece. If you are trying to make a story from various sound bites, assign a color to each topic and color-code the segments. Now you can drag them around so that each topic is grouped together or plays off of another topic.

Track of a Different Color

Not too fond of the default colors of your tracks? If you like, you can customize your track colors to mean something more significant to the content of the individual tracks. For example, in audio tracks you may want to use different colors to distinguish sound-on-tape, music, sound effects, room tone, etc. Just select the appropriate tracks, go to the Timeline Fast Menu in the lower-left corner, and choose a track color. You can change the color of any selected track, including the timecode track. If you want a color that's not in the palette, hold Alt (Option), choose any track color, and your operating system's color picker will open to allow you to choose any color your computer can display. Note: To avoid confusion, don't choose a color that is similar to the highlight color of Show Marked Region or Segment Mode.

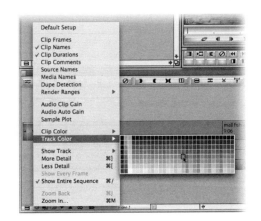

Zoom Me Up, Zoom Me Down

The scale bar at the bottom of the Timeline window is great for zooming in and out of your sequence, but that involves using the mouse. There's got to be a better way, right? As an Avid power user, you'll want to be able to zoom in and out by using the keyboard: The down arrow will zoom in and the up arrow will zoom out of your sequence, and both commands keep the blue bar position indicator centered in the window. Ctrl+[and] (Cmd+[and]) work the same way. Also, Ctrl+/ (Cmd+/) will fit the sequence in the Timeline window regardless of your current zoom level.

Ready ... Set ... Zoom!

What if you are viewing the segments in your sequence at a comfortable zoom level, and you want to zoom in a little further but eventually return to your previous zoom level? Zoom In and Zoom Back allow you to do just that. Press Ctrl+M (Cmd+M) to activate the Zoom In command. Think "M" as in "magnify." When Zoom In is active, you can lasso a region of your sequence to zoom into that region. To return to your previous zoom level, activate the Zoom Back command. Press Ctrl+J (Cmd+J). Think "J" as in "jump back." You can even magnify multiple times in a row and jump back to each previous zoom level.

Red Alert

From the Fast Menu in the lower-left corner of the Timeline, enable Clip Color>Offline so that any offline segments in your sequence will be a bright red color. This way, whenever you open a sequence, the Avid will immediately indicate that you have offline media, and you'll know which clips to relink or recapture. Note: To avoid confusion, don't tag any source or local colors with red. Perhaps most importantly, however, if you're working on a shared system and all of your segments are showing up as bright red, then you've got some detective work to do, because it's possible that somebody else deleted all of your media! Save this setting with all of your Timeline views, and you'll always know.

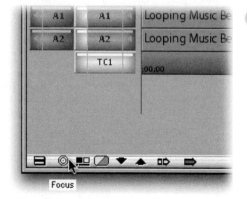

Hocus Focus

For zooming in and out the sequence, we love the scale bar at the bottom of the Timeline window, as well as using the up and down arrows or Ctrl+[and] (Cmd+[and]), but wouldn't it be nice to zoom in and out at very far levels by toggling only one button? You can quickly zoom in and out of the sequence by clicking the Focus button in the lower-left corner of the Timeline. The Focus button, a prime candidate for keyboard mapping, zooms in at a scale of 90 pixels per second (or 3 pixels per frame); press it again to return to your previous level.

Size Matters

What's the point of displaying clip information in the Timeline if the tracks are too small to read it? Enlarging your video and audio tracks creates space to display additional data, such as Clip Durations, Audio Auto Gain, or Sample Plot. To resize the height of individual tracks, move your mouse below each track until it changes into arrows, and then drag. To enlarge multiple tracks, select them, and press Ctrl+L (Cmd+L). Think "L" as in "enLarge." To shrink multiple tracks, select them, and press Ctrl+K (Cmd+K). Think "K" as in "shrinK."

A Room with a Timeline View

You can customize and save different Timeline views to use for different editing purposes. For example, you may want to save a Timeline view for audio editing that will display tall audio tracks, audio auto gain, and sample plot. Also, you may want to save a Timeline view for video editing with source, local, and offline clip colors, and a larger Timeline font. (Change the default font by activating the Timeline, and choosing Edit>Set Font.) To save a Timeline view, click on the View Menu at the bottom of the Timeline, choose "Save As," and name it appropriately. Once a view is saved, you can click on the View Menu to toggle to different views. Alt+ or Option+click to replace existing Timeline views.

Consider the Source

Have you ever wanted to see the sample plot of a clip in the Source Monitor in order to mark In and Out points? Just click the Toggle Source/Record in Timeline button in the lower left to view the source material in the Timeline. Turn on the sample plot, and you're in business. This feature can also be especially useful if you have another sequence loaded in the Source Monitor, and you need to see its edits in order to mark In and Out points at specific head and tail frames. The Toggle Source/Record in Timeline button works with footage in pop-up monitors, too.

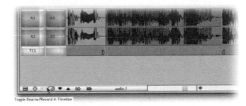

A Detective Story ⟨Pro Special⟩

Have you already used that footage on your Timeline? Choosing the Fast Menu in the lower-left corner of the Timeline and selecting Dupe Detection will draw little colored lines on the tops of the frames that you've already used. Dupe Detection was originally designed for editing film because it can be expensive to duplicate the same frame of film. You can also use this feature to your benefit to double-check that you haven't used those frames somewhere else. Note, however, that Dupe Detection only works in the V1 track.

Back in Black

Need to add black at the end of your Timeline? By default, you can only add black at the end of your sequence during a Digital Cut, but there are ways to fool the system into doing it in your Timeline:

❶ Add a title with no words.

❷ Add an audio clip with its gain turned all the way down.

❸ On an empty track at the end of the Timeline, click Add Edit. Then, enter Trim Mode, and add frames to the existing filler on the A side.

Filmstrip for You

Like to see exactly what the Timeline frames are? Go to the Fast Menu in the lower-left corner of the Timeline and choose Show Track>Film Track. This feature is normally off to save valuable Timeline height, but now you have a view to see the actual frames on your Timeline.

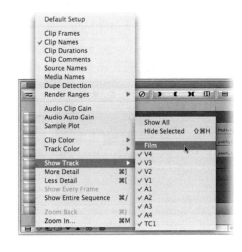

Wrap-Around Blues

When you have few or short tracks, you may find that zooming into your sequence causes it to wrap around the Timeline window, which can be quite annoying. Just make sure your tracks are tall enough, and it will defeat this wrap-around feature.

ON THE SPOT

Organization

Most creative people are also messy people, and Avid editors are some of the filthiest people in the industry. But, hope is not lost, and there is always room for improvement. These tips will help you develop better organizational habits–at least whenever you are in front of an Avid. Not only is cleanliness next to godliness, but it will make you more efficient as well. If you ever find yourself in the unfortunate but all too common situation in which the client or producer wants to supervise your editing, you will want to impress them with your excellent media hygiene. Keeping everything squeaky clean will make everything easier to find and thus turn you into a more proficient editor. So, get yourself "organazized." It will help you to think straight.

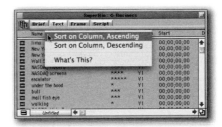

Papa's Got a Brand New Bin

Maybe it seems obvious, but people still forget to make separate bins for different clips, sequences, titles, effects, imports, music, etc., and different bins can be organized further by making folders. The SuperBin feature, which is on by default, is meant to minimize your screen space by putting all of your open bins in one window. Single-click a bin in the Project window to open it in the SuperBin. Double-click a bin to open it in a separate window. Right-click (or Ctrl+Shift+click on a one-button mouse) to close or delete a bin in the SuperBin. While this may be a handy organizational tool, it can sometimes interfere, or it may be unnecessary if you have plenty of screen real estate. You can disable the SuperBin feature from the Bin settings in the Project window.

Match Frame Made in Heaven

Imagine that you have a segment in your sequence, and you need to load its original clip in the Source Monitor but you don't have the time to look for its bin. Just park on the segment, make sure it's the topmost selected track, and click the Match Frame button. The Match Frame command loads the original clip, parks on the same frame, and automatically marks a new In point at that frame. If you don't want the Avid to mark a new In point in the source clip, hold the Alt (Option) key while clicking the Match Frame button.

A Good Bin Is Hard to Find

Imagine that you have a clip in the Source Monitor and you need to quickly find its bin. If the Source Monitor is active, the Find Bin button will automatically open the clip's bin from the Project window. How about the bin of a sequence? If the Record Monitor is active with a sequence, the Find Bin button will automatically open the sequence's bin. With the sequence's blue bar position indicator parked over a clip, hold the Alt (Option) key, click the Find Bin button, and the bin of the clip of the topmost selected track will open.

Locators, Locators, Locators

Locators allow you to leave notes for yourself in a clip or sequence.

❶   Click the Add Locator button, and a colored dot appears on the current frame of the topmost selected track. This is the film cutter's equivalent to the grease mark.

❷   Click the colored dot on the Source or Record Monitor, and the Locators window appears where you can type a comment.

❸   Holding down the Alt (Option) key while clicking the Add Locator button will add a locator and open the Locators window. (It works with the timecode track, too.)

If you map the Add Locator button to your keyboard, you can add them on the fly while playing a clip or sequence. Most commonly, editors will map the red Add Locator button to the F3 or F5 key. So now, whenever you need to add a note about an edit decision, lines from a script, or instructions for titles or effects work, just add a locator.

Headings out to the Highway

In a bin's Text View, move some statistical columns aside, and type in your own custom headings in the blank space left behind. Custom headings must be shorter than 30 characters. Once you make a custom heading, type in your clip criteria below. While entering clip data, pressing

- Enter moves down to the next line

- Shift+Enter moves up to the previous line

- Tab moves to the next column to the right

- Shift+Tab moves to the previous column to the left

Hold the Alt (Option) key and click an empty field to choose from a list of previously used criteria. To clean up the bin view, go to its Fast Menu and choose Align Columns. To rename an existing heading, Alt- or Option-click it.

Bin Examination

What's the good of seeing all of a bin's statistics if you don't sort by them? In a bin's Text View, click on a heading, and press Ctrl+E (Cmd+E) to sort by that heading. Think "E" as in "examine." So, you can easily sort a bin's clips by name, duration, starting timecode, item type, on- or offline, etc. If you press Ctrl+Alt+E (Option+Cmd+E), you can sort in the opposite order. This works with custom headings as well. So with custom headings, an editor may want to sort a bin's clips according to criteria such as shot type or rank. Shift-click additional headings from left to right to perform a multilevel sort.

A Bin with a View

Once you've created and arranged all of your headings in Text View, you can save your arrangement to use at any time in any bin. Just go to the View Menu at the bottom of the bin, choose Save As, and give the bin view an appropriate name. Once a bin view is saved, you can click on the View Menu to toggle different ones. Film and Statistics are already created for you. You may want to create separate bin views that are suited for MultiCam, for ranking your clips, or for looking at comments. If you Alt- or Option-click on the View Menu, you can replace existing bin views.

Siftin' Through the Ashes

It's very common for a bin to have over 50 or 100 items. Wouldn't it be nice if there were a quick way to search for those items? In Text View, go to the bin's Fast Menu, and choose Custom Sift (a perfect candidate for keyboard mapping). After entering your search criteria, the bin will be sifted to display only items that meet those criteria. To display all of the bin items again, go to the bin's Fast Menu, and choose Show Unsifted. You can also sift by criteria from custom headings. Or, don't Show Unsifted right away, and perform multilevel sifts.

Backup Plan

It's smart to create regular backups of your sequence. It provides some history of what you've been doing as well as a "super undo" in case you take a project in a wrong direction and have the need to go back to where you started. Every half day, Alt- or Option-drag your sequence into an Old Sequences bin. Append the sequence name with usable information like the date and "morning" or "afternoon." If you ever need to step back, you'll now have a series of backup sequences in a bin.

True Colors

During the editing process, you may want to color-code some of your clips to make them easier to find, such as clips from a specific tape or clips about a particular topic. In a bin's Text View, click on the Fast Menu, choose Headings, and select Color. Now in the Color heading, you can color-code your bin items and sort or sift by these colors. Choose Pick to open your operating system's color picker, and select a custom color. Alt- or Option-click to select previously used colors. To prevent possible confusion with offline clips, avoid using red colors. How about the bin itself? With a bin window active, choose Edit>Set Bin Background to select a different bin color. Now, if your computer screen is cluttered with several open windows, your color-coded bin will be easier to identify.

Lock and Load (but not Delete)

Once in a while, particularly in collaborative environments, important clips and sequences are unintentionally deleted. How can you communicate with others (or to yourself) to prevent this? Right-click (or Ctrl+Shift+click on a one-button mouse) on selected bin items, and choose Lock Bin Selection to lock them and prevent accidental deletion. To see which items are locked, switch your bin to Text View, click on the bin's Fast Menu, choose Headings, and select Lock. (This would also add another criterion by which you can sort or sift.) Keep in mind that locking an item only prevents deletion from its bin. It does not prevent the items from being modified. So, it would still be possible to delete all of the segments of a locked sequence. To prevent modifying a sequence, select its tracks, right-click them (or Ctrl+Shift+click on a one-button mouse), and choose Lock Tracks.

A Good Clip Is Hard to Find

Have you ever needed to quickly find a clip or locator in your sequence? With the Timeline active, press Ctrl+F (Cmd+F), specify whether you want to look for locators, clip names, or other Timeline text (such as comments or source names), enter your search criteria, and the blue bar position indicator will jump to the first qualifying clip or locator. Press Ctrl+G (Cmd+G) to jump to the next clip or locator. One way to jump to different offline clips is to enable Media Names from the Timeline Fast Menu, and choose to find the Timeline Text, "offline."

Know It All With Flat View

So, you were really diligent about putting all of your bins into folders, and folders within other folders, but keeping yourself organized can slow you down, since you're always opening and closing different folders to access different bins. If you're looking for a bin but you don't know which folder it's in, you can find it easily by viewing your Project window in Flat View. From the Bins tab in the Project window, go to the Fast Menu, and choose Flat View. All of your bins will be displayed outside of their folders and sorted alphabetically. The Trash folder will disappear until Flat View is disabled.

Safe Settings

Copying settings between Avid products is possible, but not necessarily recommended. Due to differences in capabilities and versions of certain products, imported user settings may not deliver dependable, predictable results. It is recommended that you re-create your user settings from scratch whenever moving to another product or version. To assist you in re-creating your user settings by hand, Avid recommends that you print out your settings, especially your keyboard settings.

Name Game

If you were to bring home a new pet or a new baby, what's one of the first things you usually do? You name it, of course. So, whenever you create a new bin, a new clip, a new sequence, a new title, a new whatever, do you know why Avid will first highlight its name? You guessed it! It's because the system wants you to give it a new name, ideally a name that makes sense to you. Rarely do we remember the difference between Untitled Sequence.24.Copy.32 and Untitled Sequence.24.Copy.33, especially when we need to return to a project a week or even a year later. So, name everything early and appropriately!

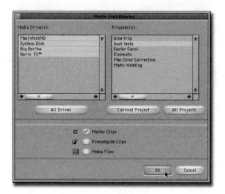

Master Bin

Another organizational method that you can add to this mix is the Master Bin method. If you want a way to sort through all of the clips in all of the bins, the answer lies in the Media tool. Go to Tools>Media Tool and choose:

- Current Project

- All Drives

- Master Clips only

- then click OK.

This will call up the Media tool filled with every clip from the current project. You can now create a new bin in your project and simply drag all of the clips from Media tool directly into your new Master Bin. (If you have added footage from other projects in your current project, make sure to include it in your master bin.)

The Tears of a Clone

There are two ways to copy a clip, but the methods you use depend on the kind of copy you want.

You can duplicate a clip by selecting it and pressing Ctrl+D (Cmd+D). This produces a new, independent clip that points to the same media. Any changes made to duplicate clips never affect the original. Whenever copying clips from someone else's bin to a bin of your own, you may want to choose this method so that you don't accidentally change the other person's clip.

If you copy a clip by Alt+ or Option+dragging it from one bin to another, you will produce a clone of the clip. Modifications to any cloned clip are reflected in all other instances of the clip. So, if you rename a cloned clip, lock it, assign it a color, or give it a comment, your changes will be made throughout the entire Avid system. This can be handy if your cloned clip is not named correctly; if you rename it once, then it will automatically be renamed everywhere else. Or, if your cloned clip is being used in several projects, locking just one will lock all of them.

Business			
Brief	Text	Frame	Script

Name	Start	Duration	Tra
telephone crush	00;00;00;00	8;03	V
limo	00;00;00;00	7;17	V
New York Stock Exchange zoom in	00;00;00;00	14;19	V
New York Stock Exchange XCU	00;00;00;00	4;19	V
Wall Street sign	00;00;00;00	6;15	V
NASDAQ tickers	00;00;00;00	29;22	V
NASDAQ screens	00;00;00;00	27;05	V
escalator	00;00;00;00	18;20	V
under the hood	00;00;00;00	15;15	V
bull	00;00;00;00	5;02	V
mall fish eye	00;00;00;00	9;06	V
walking	00;00;00;00	21;14	V
01030_VideoTraxx.mov	00;00;00;00	21;14	V
01029_VideoTraxx.mov	00;00;00;00	7;21	V
01028_VideoTraxx.mov	00;00;00;00	31;02	V
01027_VideoTraxx.mov	00;00;00;00	47;07	V
01026_VideoTraxx.mov	00;00;00;00	23;10	V

◇ Suburbia			
Brief	Text	Frame	Script

Name	Start	Duration	Tracks	Off
telephone crush	00;00;00;00	8;03	V1	
train passing by	00;00;00;00	18;08	V1	
pollution	00;00;00;00	12;10	V1	
traffic light	00;00;00;00	17;03	V1	
cityscape	00;00;00;00	18;11	V1	
station	00;00;00;00	14;15	V1	
traffic	00;00;00;00	6;21	V1	
tailgating	00;00;00;00	27;03	V1	
01180_VideoTraxx.mov	00;00;00;00	18;24	V1	
01181_VideoTraxx.mov	00;00;00;00	27;03	V1	
01182_VideoTraxx.mov	00;00;00;00	6;21	V1	
01183_VideoTraxx.mov	00;00;00;00	8;12	V1	
01184_VideoTraxx.mov	00;00;00;00	14;15	V1	
01185_VideoTraxx.mov	00;00;00;00	14;18	V1	
01186_VideoTraxx.mov	00;00;00;00	18;11	V1	
01187_VideoTraxx.mov	00;00;00;00	9;21	V1	
01188_VideoTraxx.mov	00;00;00;00	11;15	V1	

ON THE SPOT

CHAPTER 5

Getting It In

An Avid without any footage is not a particularly useful thing. You need to get your footage into the system so your creativity can be unleashed. But loading footage is about as much fun as watching chocolate chip cookies bake. All you can do is think about what you'd rather be eating (we mean doing).

The faster you can get the footage loaded, the sooner you can start editing. Learn powerful timesavers like batch recording, which can shave hours off your edit prep. In fact batch recording can give you the time you need to work in Photoshop or After Effects (or to keep reading this fine book).

You'll also learn the best way to import graphics and audio into your system. Consistency and speed are our goals, and we mean to deliver. Let's go!

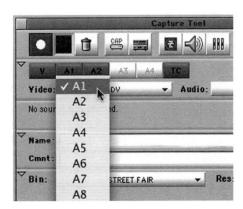

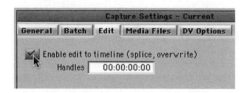

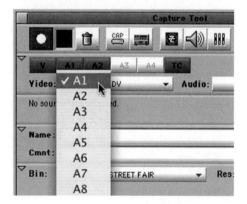

The Last Minute Bustle

The end of the edit is in sight (thank goodness), and you need to capture an extra clip to put the finishing touches on. The quickest route is always a straight line– in this case that means capturing it right to the desired point in your Timeline.

❶   In the Project window, click on the Settings tab.

❷   Scroll down to Capture and double-click it. The Capture Settings dialog appears.

❸   Click on the Edit tab.

❹   Click on the box next to "Enable edit to timeline" so a checkmark appears.

❺   Enter a handle length (we recommend 3 seconds, i.e. 00:00:03:00), and click OK.

❻   Turn on the track(s) in your sequence where you want your new clip to go.

❼   Set an In mark in your sequence where you'd like the new clip to be placed.

❽   Open the Capture Tool by selecting Tools>Capture or by using the keyboard shortcut Ctrl+7 (Cmd+7).

❾   Click and hold on the Capture Tool's track buttons for each track you wish to capture. A pop-up menu will appears in which you can select which Timeline track will be the destination for each input.

❿   Using the Capture Tool, set In and Out marks for your source clip.

⓫   Click on either the Splice Edit or Overwrite Edit button to tell Avid how to cut the new clip into your sequence.

⓬   Click the Record button.

The Avid technology captures your new clip directly to the desired place in your Timeline. You'll also find a new master clip in your bin.

Playing with a Stacked Deck (Part 1)

The Xpress Pro Capture Tool doesn't always recognize what type of camcorder or deck you have attached to it–quite often it will see it as a "Generic DV Device." It's very important that Xpress Pro knows what model of camcorder or deck you're using, as they all have their own unique characteristics. Xpress Pro's ability to capture from and record to your device depends on it knowing exactly what it's looking at. To manually select your model:

❶ Open the Capture Tool by selecting Tools>Capture or by using the keyboard shortcut Ctrl+7 (Cmd+7).

❷ Click on the pulldown menu directly below the Play button and select Adjust Deck. The Deck Settings dialog appears.

❸ From the Device pulldown menus, select your brand and model of deck.

You might find that your particular deck isn't listed. In that case, keep the Generic DV Device setting, and customize it to get more reliable performance. This might take some experimentation, but you can often get good results this way.

The current list of DV devices supported in Xpress Pro can be downloaded at www.avid.com/products/dvdevicequal.pdf.

Playing with a Stacked Deck (Part 2)

So you went ahead and made sure your deck was correctly selected, but you're still getting error messages and failures when you capture or perform a Digital Cut. Well, all decks are not created equal–the cheaper ones tend to have lower-quality mechanisms which limit the ability of Xpress Pro's deck control to operate successfully. The fine engineers at Avid HQ have tested most popular camcorders and decks and have made their findings available to you. To see what the limitations (if any) of your deck are, check the notes for your device contained within the Deck Settings dialog. In some cases, you might need to capture or perform a Digital Cut without deck control.

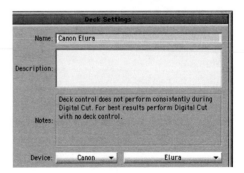

Mas   01;04;41;24

Don't Let Timecode Break You

You're logging a tape and notice that it has timecode breaks. Let's say it has three timecode breaks, so three different parts of the tape have identical timecode. It might not be a big deal to capture this, but what will happen if you need to recapture the footage at some point in the future? Xpress Pro won't know which of the three different sections of timecode to look at. An easy solution to this is to give each section of timecode its own tape name. For example, on a tape called "Tape_10" that has two timecode breaks, call the first section of timecode "Tape_10 _A," the second section "Tape_10_ B," and the third section "Tape_10_C." Make sure to include a note of this in the tape box, or on its label, to help anyone who might need to recapture down the line.

Drive Away

You'll get optimal system performance if you capture footage to drives other than those that contain your operating system and Xpress Pro program files. Your computer is constantly accessing system and application data from these drives, which leaves less bandwidth for your media. Unfortunately, Xpress Pro can't automatically tell which drives these are. To keep from accidentally capturing to those drives,

❶ In the Project window, click on the Settings tab.

❷ Scroll down to Media Creation and double-click it. The Media Creation dialog opens with the Drive Filtering tab already selected.

❸ Click the boxes next to Filter Out System Drive and Filter Out Launch Drive so they both have check-marks in them, and click OK.

Boss Your Drives Around

If you have a Mojo, you can capture to Avid's 1:1 (uncompressed) OMF format. You'll generally need a fast RAID array of drives to sustain the read/write speed necessary for uncompressed, but sometimes you can get away with using standard drives to capture short clips. The problem is that Xpress Pro automatically filters out all drives it thinks are not capable of capturing uncompressed. To override this filtering:

❶ In the Project window, click on the Settings tab.

❷ Scroll down to Media Creation and double-click it. The Media Creation dialog opens with the Drive Filtering tab already selected.

❸ Click the box next to Filter Based On Resolution so the checkmark disappears, and click OK.

Bear in mind that you might get capture errors and failures if you attempt to capture uncompressed to drives that can't handle it, but this way you'll be able to decide what works and what doesn't without having the software make the decision for you.

Tapes Can Be Flaky

The mini-DV tape format has become popular for many reasons—it's small, it's cheap, and it's widely available. What it *isn't* is durable, especially when it goes through the constant shuttling back-and-forth that occurs during capturing. For this reason, we strongly advise you to make backup copies of your master mini-DV tapes before you begin capturing into Xpress Pro. That way you'll avoid the heartbreak of losing important footage should your master tapes develop dropouts (all too common) or become completely destroyed altogether. The simplest method is to connect two camcorders or decks with a FireWire cable and do a straight dub.

Make sure to use the highest quality tape stock you can afford—the extra few bucks will be worth it in the long run. We like to use DVCAM master tapes, even in our mini-DV camcorders, because they're much more durable.

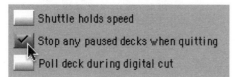

Unflattering Headwear

After a long capture session, we like to take a nice long coffee break. We love our coffee breaks so much that we often forget that we've left a tape in the deck. Even if we've quit out of Xpress Pro, that tape may very well still be threaded around our deck's playback heads. Not only will this wear down our heads, but it can also cause damage to the tape. To keep this from happening,

❶ In the Project window, click on the Settings tab.

❷ Scroll down to Deck Preferences and double-click it. The Deck Preferences dialog appears.

❸ Click on the box next to "Stop any paused decks when quitting" so a checkmark appears, and click OK.

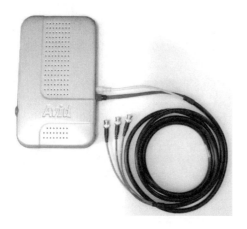

Build a Better Mojo

Mojo needs breakout cable in order to capture or play out a component video signal. Component video is of much higher quality than composite, so we consider having this cable a necessity. You can buy one from Avid for $75, but it's really easy to make your own with about $15 worth of parts from your local RadioShack. Avid's Knowledge Center website has instructions on how to do it (as well as loads of other great information).

❶ Open your web browser and type in the URL support01.avid.com.

❷ In the Search field on the upper-right-hand corner of the page, type "Mojo Component Cable" and click Go.

❸ A link to the Avid Mojo Component Cable Wiring Diagram appears. Click on it to download (it's a PDF file, so you'll need to have Adobe Reader installed to read it).

The document even includes a detailed list of the parts you'll need.

The Magic Drive Expander

On high-end Avids, the standard workflow is to capture source material at a lower-quality offline resolution and then up-rez the final sequence to a high-quality online resolution. The main reason for this is to conserve drive space. With Xpress Pro's 15:1s resolution, you can use this very same workflow to get around 10 times more footage on your drives!

One gigabyte of drive space can store:

- 48.5 minutes of 15:1s footage

- 5 minutes of DV25 footage

- 0.8 minutes of 1:1 footage

Bear in mind that you'll need to have access to your source tapes when it comes time to up-rez your sequence to DV25.

Can You Handle It?

It's always a good idea to capture source clips with handles. This means that you capture a few extra seconds at the beginning and end of each clip to give you some extra leeway in your edits. Quite often, you'll need more frames than you thought you would to get a transition exactly the way you want it. A handle length of 3 seconds (90 frames for NTSC, 75 frames for PAL) is a safe amount.

- When performing a batch capture, select Extend Handles Beyond Master Clip Edges in the Batch Capture dialog.

- When capturing clip by clip, manually capture handles by setting your In and Out marks to include extra footage at the beginning and end of the clip.

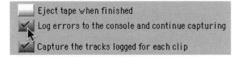

Playing Through the Pain

It's happened to us way too often—we log a tape with tons of clips on it, tell Xpress Pro to perform a batch capture, go off to lunch, and come back to find the batch capture has failed. Usually the culprit is a single clip—why let one bad apple spoil the whole batch?

❶ In the Project window, click on the Settings tab.

❷ Scroll down to Capture and double-click it. The Capture Settings dialog appears.

❸ Click on the Batch tab.

❹ Click the box next to "Log errors to the console and continue capturing" so a checkmark appears, and click OK.

Once your batch capture is complete, you'll get an error message if any clips failed to capture. You can then open the console to see all the gory details by selecting Tools>Console or by using the keyboard shortcut Ctrl+6 (Cmd+6).

We Don't Need No Stinking Tapes!

A shot log has been faxed to you . . . but the tapes still haven't arrived. Not to worry—you can still log your shots in the Capture Tool, even without having a tape in the deck. You'll need to manually enter In and Out marks in the Capture Tool, but before you do this Xpress Pro needs to know if the forthcoming tape has drop or non-drop timecode.

❶ In the Project window, click on the Settings tab.

❷ Scroll down to Deck Preferences and double-click it. The Deck Preferences dialog appears.

❸ From the "When the deck contains no tape, Log As:" pulldown menu, select "Drop Frame" or "Non-drop Frame" and click OK.

Look Sharp /Pro Special\

The DV format isn't kind to titles and graphics. They tend to fall apart when subjected to DV's 5:1 compression. If you have a Mojo, you can steer clear of all that by importing titles and graphics to Avid's uncompressed format. In fact, this is one of the key benefits of owning a Mojo in the first place.

❶ In the Project window, click on the Settings tab.

❷ Scroll down to Media Creation and double-click it. The Media Creation dialog appears.

❸ Click on the Import tab.

❹ In the Video Resolution pulldown, select 1:1, and click OK.

You can also set 1:1 in the Titles and Render tabs of the Media Creation tool to keep your Avid titles and effects renders uncompressed. If you'll be outputting to an analog format via Mojo or to MPEG-2 for DVD, your graphics, titles, and effects renders will never suffer that ugly DV 5:1 compression hit.

Yo, Shorty!

If you're short on drive space, why not import still files at a short duration? You can then cut the still into your sequence multiple times to create the desired length. This is especially useful if you're importing your stills 1:1 which eats up tons of drive space.

Single Frame Import
Duration: 10 seconds

❶ In the Project window, click on the Settings tab.

❷ Scroll down to Import and double-click it (if you have multiple Import settings, make sure you select the one you wish to modify).

❸ In the Single Frame Import field, enter your desired duration.

We like to use a duration of 10 seconds, which is easy to multiply.

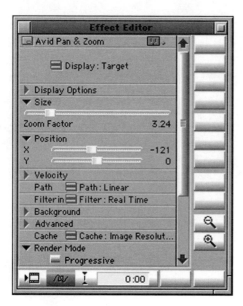

Your Virtual Animation Stand

It's common to "pan and scan" still photos to zoom in on points of interest. It's also more interesting to watch than a still photo just sitting there doing nothing. Don't use the standard File>Import for this, as Xpress Pro will reduce your beautiful high-res image to DV frame size. Import it with the Avid Pan & Zoom effect instead.

❶ Access the Effects Palette by clicking on the Project window's Effects tab.

❷ In the left-hand column, scroll down to Image and click it. The Avid Pan & Zoom effect appears at the top of the right-hand column.

❸ Drag the Avid Pan & Zoom effect to an empty area in the desired video track in your sequence. Filler is created with the effect applied to it.

❹ Park the position marker over the filler containing the Pan & Zoom effect.

❺ Open the Effect Editor by selecting Tools>Effect Editor.

❻ Click on the box in the upper-left corner of the Effect Editor window, directly to the left of the words "Avid Pan & Zoom." In the dialog that appears, select the image file you wish to import, and click OK.

❼ Click on the Avid Pan & Zoom effect's Display pulldown menu, and select Display:Target.

Set keyframes to animate Size and Position over time, and you can create a visually stimulating pan and scan, while zooming in on the finest detail.

Note that Xpress Pro doesn't create media for your still as it would if you used the standard File>Import command. OMF media for the effect will be created when you render, but if you want to be able to make changes, make sure to keep your original image file handy. Your photo needs to be bigger than screen size if you inted to pan and zoom. The television screen is 720 pixels wide, so if you want to do a four-time zoom or pan just do the math ($4 \times 720 = 2880$ pixels wide).

I've Been Converted

Your Xpress Pro project will almost always have an audio sample rate of 48kHz or 32kHz, but audio tracks on CDs have a sample rate of 44.1kHz. You can import them at 44.1kHz and they'll play back just fine in your sequence, but when it comes time to output you'll have to convert them to your project sample rate. When importing tracks from CDs, always click Yes when Xpress Pro asks you if you want to perform the sample rate conversion. The sample rate conversion makes the import slower, but it'll save you from having to do it later on.

On the other hand, you might have an impatient client sitting next to you, and taking the time to convert a big batch of tracks might not be realistic. In this case, click No to the sample rate conversion and do it later on when things aren't so hectic.

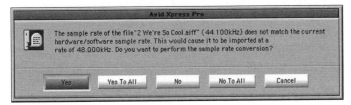

Mojo's Stealth Multitasking

Mojo outputs your After Effects composition window to a broadcast monitor! When you launch After Effects on Windows it will display your comp window through Mojo's analog and FireWire outputs. Just hook your monitor up to Mojo and you're all set.

Mac users need not despair. You can also get After Effects comp window output to a broadcast monitor by setting the Output Device to FireWire in the Video Preview section of After Effects Preferences dialog. In order to connect an analog monitor, you'll need to have a FireWire-to-analog converter attached to your FireWire port.

In general, it's a good idea to preview your After Effects comp on a broadcast monitor as what you see on your computer screen is never an accurate representation of what it's going to look like on a television.

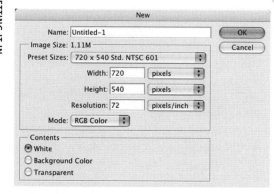

Be Still, My Beating Heart

If you need to incorporate still photos or graphics into your Xpress Pro or Xpress DV edit, then Adobe Photoshop is a must-have. One thing you need to be aware of is that Avid uses non-square pixels, while Photoshop and other graphics tools usually use square pixels.

When you create a still or graphic in Photoshop and import it into an Avid system, the pixels will be reinterpreted. If you build the graphic at the same size of your video frame (720×486 or 720×480), you will see a slight distortion. There are several approaches to solving this problem (and a lot of misinformation floating around). Here's a workflow that works well for NTSC.

❶ Create your still graphic using the following sizes

  • 640×486 pixels for Standard D1 video

  • 640×480 pixels for DV projects

❷ While the Avid can resize the graphic, it better to do this in Photoshop.

❸ Choose Image>Image Size.

❹ Uncheck the Constrain Proportions box.

❺ Resize your image to the finished video size:

  • 720×486 pixels for Standard D1 video

  • 720×480 pixels for DV projects

❻ Choose File>Save As and save your file as a PICT or TARGA if you don't need layers to import. Save a layered PSD file as well.

Be sure to work in the RGB colorspace. The good news if you've upgraded to Photoshop CS, you don't need to go through these steps because it's the first version of Photoshop that lets you create images with nonsquare pixels. Just use the built in templates.

You're Still My PAL

❶ Create your still graphic using the following size (PAL uses the same frame size for both Standard and Digital Video).

- 768×576 pixels

❷ While the Avid can resize the graphic, it better to do this in Photoshop.

❸ Choose Image>Image Size.

❹ Uncheck the Constrain Proportions box.

❺ Resize your image to the finished video size to 720×576 pixels

❻ Choose File>Save As and save your file as a PICT or TARGA if you don't need layers to import. Save a layered PSD file as well.

Rules of Capture

If you choose to turn the Deck button off while you are recording, you can still get video into the system (but not much more).

❶ You cannot uprez from a lower resolution because there is no way for Xpress Pro to find the original source.

❷ If a clip becomes damaged, you'll have no way to reload it and have it sync up in the timeline. Without a timecode reference any data acquired could easily become lost.

❸ Without timecode, it'll be hard to properly search through your bins.

❹ Perhaps more importantly, any capturing errors that occurs could prove devastating.

Your Comments, Please?

As you log your clips in the Capture Tool, take advantage of Avid technology's ability to add comments.

- Enter notes on the type of shot (e.g. interior, exterior, b-roll).

- For sound bites, enter the first and last bits of dialogue for easily locating later on.

- Enter the name of the person on camera in case you need to create lower-thirds (titles with the subject's name).

- Enter comments a producer is throwing at you as you're capturing.

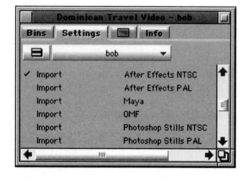

Drop It!

You can import material into Xpress Pro by dragging it from a folder to any open bin. Before you do this, you need to make sure the Import settings are properly set for the type of material you are importing. Instead of having to modify the settings each time you import, set up a different Import setting for each type of material.

❶ In the Project window click on the Settings tab.

❷ Click on Import to highlight it.

❸ Select Edit>Duplicate, or use the keyboard shortcut Ctrl+D (Cmd+D). A new Import setting appears in the Settings window.

❹ Double-click on the new Import setting. The Import Settings dialog appears.

❺ Set the parameters for the type of material this setting will apply to and click OK.

❻ Click in the column to the right of the new Import setting. A cursor appears. Type in a meaningful name for this setting and press Return.

To activate your Import setting of choice, click in the column to the left of that setting. A checkmark appears, indicating that it's now the active setting.

Duck and Cover

One of the things we love about Xpress Pro is its project compatibility with high-end Avid systems. But what if you need to import a Final Cut Pro project into Xpress Pro? The project files are incompatible. It might seem like you're out of luck, but you can always reach for the duck–Automatic Duck, that is. This neat utility can convert a Final Cut Pro project to Xpress Pro and vice versa. It can also be used to import projects to After Effects and Boris RED. We'd be lost without our duck. Check it out at www.automaticduck.com.

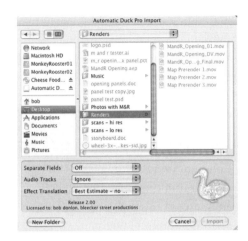

A Fresh New Batch

Even though Xpress Pro and Final Cut Pro have many incompatibilities, solutions keep appearing that help editors transition projects from one to the other. For example, if someone gives you a Final Cut Pro batch list for a tape, you won't be able to import it into Xpress Pro because Avid uses a different log format (Avid Log Exchange, or ALE). You can, however, convert your FCP batch list to an ALE file by using a utility called Sebsky Tools. Not only does it work like a charm, but it's also free! Download your copy at www.dharmafilm.com/sebskytools and add it to your digital toolbox.

Avoid Camera Burnout

It's great that Xpress Pro and DV lets you use your DV camcorder as if it were a deck—you can capture from it and you can record to it. The only problem is that camcorders aren't designed to be used as decks. The constant shuttling that's required during the capture process wears down the components of the camcorder rather quickly, decreasing its lifespan. If you plan on doing a considerable amount of capturing, we strongly recommend investing in a tape deck. Not only will it capture more reliably than a camcorder, it will save you from having to run out and buy a new camera sooner than you'd planned on!

A decent mini-DV tape deck can be bought for around $700, and for $1,200-$1,500 you can get something really nice that handles both mini-DV and DVCAM tapes. One of the most costly components of a camcorder is the lens—with that out of the equation you get good bang for the buck.

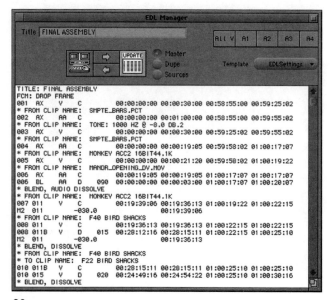

An Ounce of Prevention

It's always important to remain aware of where your project is heading. If you're using Xpress Pro for offline editing, chances are you'll be exporting an EDL (Edit Decision List) for the system that will be used in the online edit. Much online work is still done with traditional tape-to-tape editing systems, and these systems often have stiff requirements for how the EDL is set up. Why are we telling you this in a chapter about capturing and importing? Well, one common EDL "gotcha" is that many online systems have a naming convention for tape and clip names. If you log your footage in Xpress Pro and you're not following the online system's naming convention, you'll find yourself with a lot of extra work down the line. Pick up the phone and talk to your online facility to see how their system likes tapes and clips to be named.

The More, the Merrier

If you've got multiple tape decks attached to your Xpress Pro system, use the Deck Configuration setting to create a site configuration. That way, you'll be able to toggle between your decks by making a single menu pick in the Capture tool.

❶ In the Project window, click on the Settings tab.

❷ Scroll down to Deck Configuration and double-click it.

❸ Click the Add Channel button. The Channel selection dialog appears.

❹ Select the deck's input Channel Type and Port by using the pulldown menus, and click OK. A dialog appears asking if you want to autoconfigure the channel. Click No.

❺ Click the Add Deck button. The Deck Settings dialog appears.

❻ Select the deck type by using the Device pulldown menus, and click OK.

❼ Repeat steps 3 thru 6 for each additional deck.

❽ If you'd like Xpress Pro to test your new configuration, click the box next to "Verify configuration against actual decks" so a checkmark appears.

❾ Click Apply.

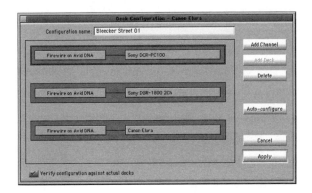

Now when you open the Capture tool, all of your decks will appear in the pulldown menu directly beneath the Play button.

Too Much Togetherness

It's very common to use similar names when naming your graphic files. However, when Autodetect Sequential Files is turned on during an import, and if there are two files with sequential numbers, they will be imported as a clip together, with each graphic represented by only a single frame. The lesson here is to always check your import options.

The After Effects Express

Adobe After Effects is an ideal compositing tool to use in conjunction with Xpress Pro. This tip provides you with the basic info you need to create and render your After Effects compositions for optimal importing into Xpress Pro. The three things you need to set correctly within After Effects are Composition Settings, Render Settings, and Output Module.

Composition Settings

- If you're working in NTSC, and your Xpress Pro project is DV, set your comps to NTSC DV, 720×480 with a pixel aspect ratio of D1/DV NTSC (0.9).

- If you're working in NTSC with a Mojo and wish to keep your After Effects renders uncompressed (which we highly recommend), set your comps to NTSC D1, 720×486 with a pixel aspect ratio of D1/DV NTSC (0.9).

- If you're working in PAL, set your comps to PAL D1/DV, 720×576 with a pixel aspect ratio of D1/DV PAL (1.07).

- Set your frame rate to 29.97fps for NTSC or 25fps for PAL.

- All of these settings are available by choosing your fotrmat from the Preset list.

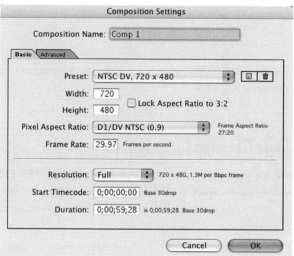

Render Settings

- Set Field Render to Lower Field First for NTSC.

- Set Field Render to Upper Field First for PAL (or Lower Field First for PAL DV).

You can save these settings as a template by clicking on the triangle next to the setting name in the render queue

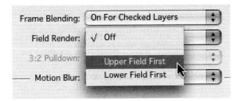

Output Module

- Set Format to QuickTime Movie.

- Set Channels to RGB if you don't need to include an alpha channel, or RGB + Alpha if you do.

- Set depth to Millions of Colors if you're not including an alpha channel, or Millions of Colors+ if you are.

- If you're including an alpha channel, set Color to Straight (Unmatted).

- Click Format Options to open the Compression Settings dialog, and set the output codec to Animation with Depth set to Millions of Colors and Quality set to Best. If you're including an alpha channel set Depth to Millions of Colors+.

- Don't change the frame rate in the Compression Settings dialog.

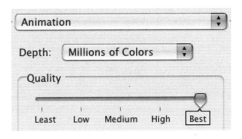

We recommend rendering to the Animation codec as it provides noticeably better image quality than the Avid DV or Avid Meridien Uncompressed codecs (especially if your comp includes gradients). You can save these settings as a template by clicking on the triangle next to the setting name in the render queue.

After After Effects

Now that you know how to set up and render your After Effects compositions, here's what you need to know to import them into Xpress Pro:

❶   In the Project window, click on the Settings tab.

❷   Scroll down to the currently active (checkmarked) Import setting and duplicate it by clicking on it once to highlight it, then selecting Edit>Duplicate.

❸   Give your new Import setting a meaningful name, like "After Effects Import" by clicking in the field to the right of it and typing in a name.

❹   Double-click on your new After Effects Import setting to open its Import Settings dialog.

❺   Apply the following settings by clicking on the circle next to the name of the setting:

- Set Aspect Ratio, Pixel Aspect to 601, non-square.

- Set Color Levels to RGB unless your After Effects comp has gradients in which case set it to RGB, dithered.

- Set File Field Order to match the field order you set in your After Effects Render Settings.

- Set Alpha to Ignore if your After Effects output doesn't contain an alpha channel, or to Invert Existing if it does.

❻   Click OK to close the Import Settings dialog.

When you are ready to import your After Effects rendered files, make sure your new Import setting is selected by clicking to the left of it in the Project window Settings tab so a checkmark appears. You can then use the File>Import command or drag and drop your After Effects renders into a bin.

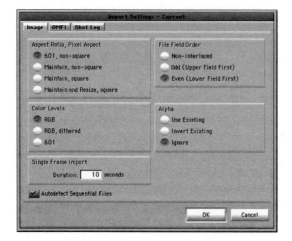

The Golden Voiceover (Part 1)

Turn Xpress Pro into a virtual voiceover studio by using the Audio Punch-In tool to record directly to your Timeline. If you're recording voiceover to sync with picture, there's really no better way. First you need to connect a microphone to your Xpress Pro system and set its input channel and level.

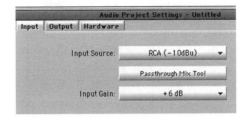

❶ Connect your microphone to your Xpress Pro system in one of three ways:

- Via Mojo's analog audio input.
- Via FireWire through your DV deck/camcorder or an analog-to-firewire converter.
- To your computer's sound card.

❷ In the Project window, click on the Settings tab.

❸ Double-click on Audio Project. The Audio Project Settings dialog appears.

❹ Click on the Input tab.

❺ Use the Input Source pulldown to select your microphone's input channel.

- If it's connected via Mojo's analog input, select RCA (-10dBu).
- If it's connected via FireWire, select OHCI.
- If it's connected to your computer's sound card, select Line In.

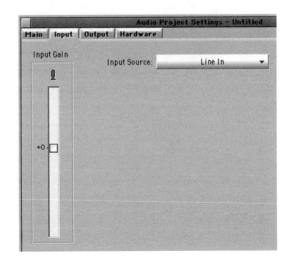

❻ Open the Audio Tool by selecting Tools>Audio Tool, or use the keyboard shortcut Ctrl+1 (Cmd+1).

❼ Set your Audio Tool to monitor your microphone's input by clicking on its In/Out buttons so they read I (for input).

❽ As your voiceover talent speaks into the microphone, adjust the input level while monitoring the meters in your Audio Tool. They should peak around –12db.

- If you're using Mojo, click the Passthrough Mix Tool button and adjust the input level in the Passthrough Mix Tool.
- If you're not using Mojo, use the Input Gain slider to adjust the input level.

Now you're ready to begin recording your voiceover. The next part of this tip tells you how.

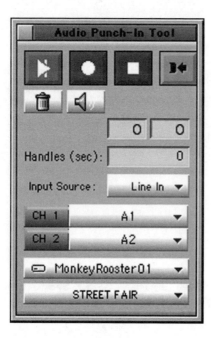

The Golden Voiceover (Part 2)

With your microphone connected and your input channel and level set (as described in Part 1 above):

❶ Set In and Out marks to select the portion of your sequence that you'll be recording voiceover for.

❷ Open the Audio Punch-In Tool by selecting Tools>Audio Punch-In.

❸ In the Audio Punch-In Tool, select the input channel for your microphone by clicking on its Input Channel button so it turns purple.

- If your mic is attached to the left channel, select CH1.

- If it's attached to the right channel, select CH2.

- If it's a stereo mic, select both channels.

❹ Assign the Timeline track(s) your voiceover will be recorded to by using the pulldown menus to the right of each Input Channel button.

❺ Select a destination drive and bin for your incoming audio clip by using the pulldown menus at the bottom of the Audio Punch-In Tool.

❻ Click the Audio Punch-In Tool's Record button, and away you go.

Avid plays the section of your sequence within the In and Out marks as it records in real-time from your microphone.

It's a good idea to have a lead-in so your sequence starts playing a few seconds before the audio punch-in takes place. This gives your talent some time to get oriented before recording starts. To specify a lead-in duration, enter it (in seconds) in the Audio Punch-In Tool Preroll field, which is the left-hand box directly above the Handles field. You can use the Postroll field to the right to enter a lead-out duration as well.

Your Virtual Logging Assistant (Part 1)

Most DV camcorders time-stamp your tape whenever the record button is pushed. Xpress Pro's DV Scene Extraction feature can use this time-stamp information to automatically create subclips and add locators for you. It creates a new subclip and/or locator wherever the record button was pushed, so in many instances it can save you from having to manually log and capture each clip.

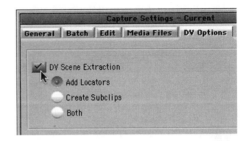

❶   In the Project window, click on the Settings tab.

❷   Scroll down to Capture and double-click it. The Capture Settings dialog appears.

❸   Click on the DV Options tab.

❹   Click on the box next to DV Scene Extraction so a checkmark appears.

❺   Click to select Add Locators, Create Subclips, or Both, and click OK.

You'll get maximum efficiency by capturing entire tapes (or large sections thereof) in a single pass. Your resulting subclips will appear in the same bin that you capture your master clip to.

Your Virtual Logging Assistant (Part 2)

If your footage is already captured, don't despair. You can also use DV Scene Extraction on clips already captured to a bin.

❶   Select your clip in its bin.

❷   Select Bin>DV Scene Extraction. The DV Scene Extraction dialog appears.

❸   Click to select Add Locators, Create Subclips, or Both.

❹   If you have Create Subclips or Both selected, select the target bin for your subclips in the "Create subclips in" pulldown menu and click OK.

Locators (if selected) are added to your master clip, and subclips (if selected) are placed in your specified bin.

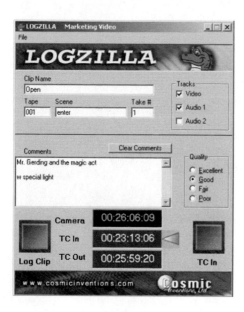

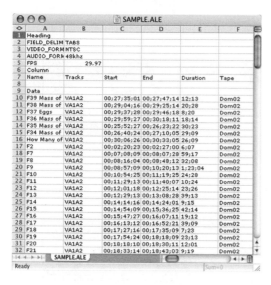

Captain's Log

If called on to attend a shoot in the field (or if you're the one doing the shooting), get a head start on editing by logging the tapes on the set. If it's not feasible to do it at the shoot, take advantage of any time you might have while sitting in your hotel room, on the plane ride home, or waiting for the plane ride home. We bring a laptop with Xpress Pro loaded on it to every shoot, along with a small, cheap DV camcorder and log our tapes that way. You can also log with any ALE-compliant logging software, such as Avid Medialog (www.avid.com), Logzilla (www.logzilla.com), or DV Log (www.imagineproducts.com).

Spreadsheet software, such as Microsoft Excel, can also work in a pinch. You can use it to manually type in clip names, start and end timecodes, and any other info you wish. Just make sure the columns in the spreadsheet are ALE compliant. Not sure how? Export an ALE file from Xpress Pro and open it in your spreadsheet to see how it looks:

❶ In Xpress Pro, highlight any bin which contains master clips, and select File>Export.

❷ In the Export Bin As dialog, set a name and destination for your ALE file and click OK.

❸ Launch your spreadsheet application and select File>Open.

❹ Navigate to your ALE file and open it. Pay attention to any dialogs that ask how you want the file opened, and make sure to select "tab delimited" or "delimited."

Once you see how the file is formatted, delete the data from each column and save the spreadsheet as a template.

A Refreshing Pause

When you click the Mark Out or Mark Out & Log button in the Capture tool, your camcorder/deck continues playing your tape. It's often necessary to enter a clip name and comments *after* setting an Out mark. While you're doing this the tape keeps on playing, and you usually need to rewind to set the In mark on the next clip. On a tape with lots of short clips, this could amount to a whole lot of rewinding, which wears down both tape and deck. Tell Xpress Pro to pause your deck when you set your Out Mark and avoid all that rewinding:

❶   In the Project window, click on the Settings tab.

❷   Scroll down to Capture and double-click it. The Capture Settings dialog appears.

❸   Click in the box next to Pause deck while logging so a checkmark appears, and click OK.

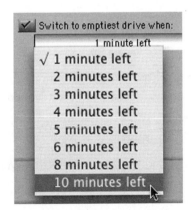

Next time you log using the Capture tool, you'll notice that the Mark Out & Log button has been replaced with a Mark Out button.

Don't Fill 'Er Up

Just like it's a bad idea to top off the tank on your car, it's a bad idea to fill your drives completely. We recommend keeping at least 5-10 percent of the drive empty. Failure to do so could negatively affect the performance of the drive and even lead to data loss. Xpress Pro can keep you from topping off your drives by automatically switching to another drive when the drive you're capturing to is nearing its limit.

❶   In the Project window, click on the Settings tab.

❷   Scroll down to Capture and double-click it. The Capture Settings dialog appears.

❸   Click on the Media Files tab.

❹   Click in the box next to "Switch to emptiest drive when:" so a checkmark appears.

❺   From the pulldown menu, select "10 minutes left."

Ten minutes is really too little, but it's the highest value Xpress Pro allows. It's better to keep an eye on your drives yourself, but at least now you won't go too far into the danger zone when your attention is focused elsewhere.

ON THE SPOT

Picture Perfect

Color correction is not just correcting colors. If that's all it was, it would still be one impressive tool! But, color correction offers you the power to grab your audience from the very first frame and hold them riveted on your story until the last frame.

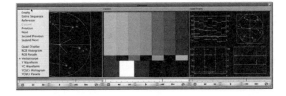

Color correction can drive the emotions of your story. They can actually help you tell your story and it can help keep your audience in your story. Often, color correction is discussed as some black art that the uninitiated had best not attempt, but this chapter will reveal the secrets and shed light on a powerful tool that can deliver much more than you ever expected. Plus the interface is really cool, and pushing pixels around can be just plain fun.

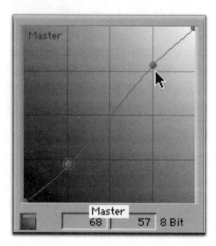

The "S" Curve Instant Makeover!

One of the fastest ways to make almost any picture look better is to add a very mild S curve in the Master Curve in color correction mode. This simulates the gamma curve of film. It slightly darkens the deep blacks and makes the highlights sparkle.

1 Choose Toolset>Color Correction to go to the Color Correction Toolset. Click on the Curves tab with a typical video image in the current monitor.

2 Click about a quarter of the way up from the bottom of the diagonal line and drag the point slightly downward.

3 Click about a quarter of the way down from the top of the diagonal line and drag the point slightly upward.

4 If it looks better, you're done. If not, then experiment a bit or undo by Alt+clicking (Option+clicking) on the small button under the left corner of the master tab. This resets it to the factory defaults. You can also toggle back and forth between seeing your correction and seeing the unaffected video by clicking on this button.

The Matching Game

You can match an on-screen video color to your computer's color picker, for example matching a logo in a shot to a Pantone color. You should note that there are three different color correction tabs where this match can be made and they will all give you slightly different results based on your video image. Try your match in each tab.

❶ In the Color Correction Toolset, in either the HSL Controls or Hue Offsets tab or in the Curves tab, there are two color swatches to the far right of the tab. If you hover your mouse over this button for a few seconds it will call up an identifier that says, "Select a Color to be Changed in the Current Monitor." Click on this color swatch and drag up to the spot on your current monitor that you want to match.

❷ Now, double-click on the color swatch to the right. This calls up the color picker. The color pickers on PCs and Macs look quite different but basically do the same thing. Type in either the HSL numbers, the RGB numbers, or even the CMYK numbers that you want to match and click OK.

All of these color spaces—YUV, RGB, CMYK—map colors a little differently, so the color may be shifted slightly and some colors that exist in one color space do not exist in the others.

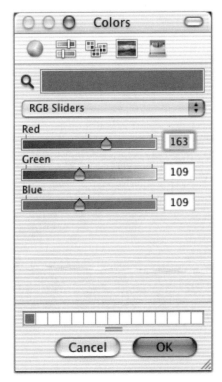

I Need to Save a Bucket

If you have created the perfect color correction and want to apply it to other shots, Color Buckets are the answer. Color Buckets are the four buttons in the bottom-right corner of all of the Color Correction tabs.

❶   To save a finished color correction to a color bucket, Alt-click (Opt-click) on the empty button above C1. This saves the correction to that button.

❷   Now, to apply the correction to another shot, make sure the shot is in the current monitor (typically the center one) and click on the C1 button (not the little diagonal color bars button above it).

Second Sight

While Avid Xpress Pro does not appear to include any secondary color correction tools, you can fake it by using the RGBKeyer.

❶   Edit the same clip on top of itself in V1 and V2.

❷   On the V2 clip, apply an RGBKeyer from the Key category.

❸   For your key color, select the color you want to isolate, and adjust the Gain, Soft, Blur, and Erode parameters appropriately. Hint: Toggle the Show Alpha button to get a better sense of your selection.

❹   Enable the Color Correction controls to adjust the areas outside of your selection. Alternatively, click the Reverse button to adjust only the selection.

Mapping Buckets to Your Keyboard

The fastest way to apply the corrections that are saved in your Color Buckets is if you map them to your keyboard.

❶ In the Settings tab of your Project window double-click on the Keyboard setting. This calls up a representation of your keyboard.

❷ Call up the Command Palette from Tools>Command Palette or by using Ctrl+3 (Cmd+3).

❸ With the "Button to Button Reassignment" button active (at the bottom left of the Command Palette) go to the CC tab of the Command Palette and drag all four color bucket buttons (the ones labeled C1-C4) to keys on your keyboard.

❹ Close the Keyboard setting window and the Command Palette. Now when you are in Color Correction mode, you will be able to apply whatever corrections are saved to those buckets by pressing the corresponding keys that you just mapped.

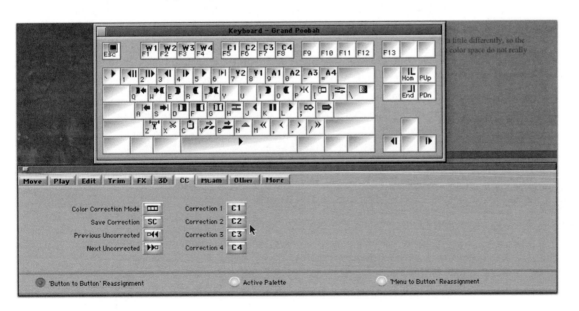

Show and Tell

You may want to show your client several different color correction options for a single shot. Or you may just want to experiment a little and compare several different correction approaches yourself. It's easiest to judge these corrections by looking at them in fairly quick succession. Color buckets is a great way to run these comparisons. When you are satisfied with each of your color correction experiments, save them to the color buckets (as explained in Saving and Applying Color Buckets) and then toggle through your choices (possibly using the tip in Mapping Buckets to your Keyboard) to see which one is best.

Saving Corrections to a Bin

If you run out of buckets, you can save corrections by dragging them to your bins where they will be saved just like a clip. You can either drag corrections from your buckets or, in the upper-right corner of the color correction tool, there is a small color correction effect button. In either instance, you drag the rectangular button with the diagonal color bars directly to a bin. When it's in the bin, you can name it something descriptive to help you remember where to apply it. This could be a simple description of what you did to it, like "lowered gamma," or a description of the shot it's designed for, like "Jones' interview in office."

Checking Your Color Correction Work

All of the tabs and parameters of the Color Correction tool interact with each other. In order to see if the corrections you are making in your current tab or parameter are helping or hurting, you can toggle off the effect that just that parameter is producing without undoing the rest of the color correction work in the other parameters. To the left of each parameter or under each Hue Offset wheel or Curve are small, square buttons; toggling these off removes that parameter from the color correction mix. Each tab and subtab of the Color Correction tool also has one of these buttons so you can toggle off all the parameters in a given tab.

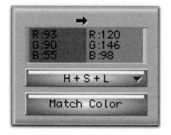

Clients Want the Strangest Things

So you're doing a correction and the client says "That's the color I want! I want the color of the grass to be the same color as the audio track in your Timeline! It's perfect!" Once you've put aside thoughts of murder, try this:

❶ In the Settings tab of your Project window, double-click the Correction setting.

❷ In the Correction Setting window, enable the "Eyedropper picks from anywhere in the application" button and click OK.

❸ Back in the Correction Tool, click on the left color swatch and drag to the grass in the current monitor and release. Then click on the right color swatch and drag down to the green audio tracks in your Timeline and release.

❹ Now click on the Match Color button under the color swatches. These color matches can work quite differently depending on the options selected in the matching menu above the Match Color button.

This tip can even let you sample a color from media in another application. For example, a photograph or graphic in Photoshop can be sampled with this method.

Eyedropper Averaging

Sometimes, due to the amount of noise in video and the size of the monitor from which you are eyedroppering, the single pixel that the eyedropper analyzes is not truly representative of the color around it. Instead it is often better to display the average of a 3x3 grid of pixels instead of a single pixel. Here's how:

❶ In the Settings tab of your Project window double click on the Correction setting.

❷ In the Correction Setting window, enable the "Eyedropper 3×3 averaging" button and click OK.

❸ Now you'll be looking at a representative average using your eyedropper.

Zoom I Zoom Do

If you want to gain even more control with your eyedropper when trying to pick colors, there are two great tips. One is that you can zoom in to your color correction monitors by clicking on them, then using Ctrl+L (Cmd+L) to zoom in, and Ctrl+K (Cmd+K) zoom back out.

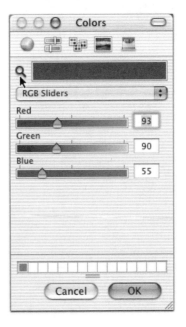

On the Mac, you can also double-click on a color swatch and use the Magnifying Glass in the color picker to pick the right pixel. Just click on the magnifying glass icon in the picker and move it over your image, and click. Then, when you're done, choose Enter (OK).

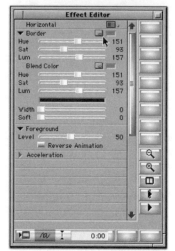

For Mac

The Color Picker can be used to share colors that you pick in color correction mode when you're in the Title Tool or other effects modes, or even outside of Xpress Pro and DV.

❶ In the Color Correction Tool, click on a color swatch in the Color Match Control area and pick a color from any monitor. (You can also pick colors directly with the Color Picker using the Magnifying Glass icon on a Mac.)

❷ Open the color picker by double-clicking on the color swatch.

❸ In the color picker, click on the large color swatch at the top and drag it to a palette button at the bottom of the color picker, then click OK.

❹ In the Title Tool, if you click and hold on a color swatch you get the Title Tool's color picker. Drag to the small bulls-eye icon to call up the main color picker and choose a color from the palette by clicking on it.

Even cooler, you can use these same colors in the Effect Editor.

❶ Add an effect, like an Edge Wipe, to a clip in your Timeline.

❷ Go into Effect mode and click on the small "options" button next to the color swatch button for the Border color. This calls up the color picker.

❸ Pick your color from the palette at the bottom and click "OK" to assign that color to the border.

For PC

The color picker can be used to share colors that you pick in Color Correction mode when you're in the Title Tool or other effects modes, or even outside of Xpress Pro.

① In the Color Correction Toolset, click on a color swatch in the Color Match Control area and pick a color from any monitor.

② Open the color picker by double clicking on the color swatch.

③ In the color picker, you can save the color you picked, which is in the Color|Solid swatch, by clicking the Add To Custom Colors button, then click OK. This adds the color to the Custom Color palette.

④ In the Title Tool, if you click and hold on a color swatch you get the Title Tool's Color Picker. Drag to the small bulls-eye icon to call up the main color picker and choose a color from the palette by clicking on it.

Even cooler, you can use these same colors in the Effect Editor.

① Add an effect, like an Edge Wipe, to a clip in your Timeline.

② Go into Effect mode and click on the small "options" button next to the color swatch button for the Border color. This calls up the color picker.

③ Pick your color from the palette at the bottom and click OK to assign that color to the border.

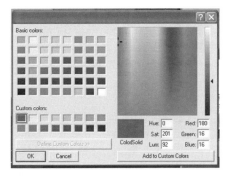

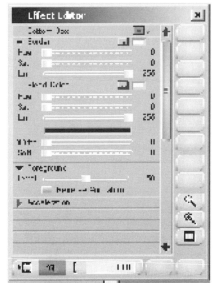

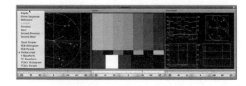

You Could Use Some Scope!

You really need scopes to do color correction. To call up the software scopes built into the Avid technology:

❶ In the Color Correction tool, in the Monitors window, at the top, each Monitor name (usually labeled Previous, Current and Next) is actually a pulldown menu called the Source Monitor Menu.

❷ Click on the name of one of these monitors to reveal the menu and pick a scope from the list. Quad display shows four of the most popular tools for video analysis in a single monitor.

❸ Usually, the Y waveform is good for determining proper luminance and the vectorscope can help with saturation and hue issues. Most serious colorists dismiss the effectiveness of some of the other tools presented here, with the exception of the RGB waveform, which can help with color casts and many other issues.

Good vs. Evil

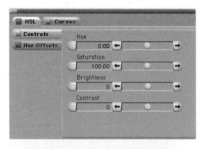

There are good ways to affect the brightness and contrast of an image and there are bad ways. As you look through the parameters of your Color Correction Toolset, you may wonder what the difference is between brightness and gain. Our opinion is that one of these is good and one is evil. In color correction, control is the most important thing. Yet when you use the brightness slider, it raises the entire video signal equally, from blacks through highlights. Gain, however, mostly operates on the highlights and leaves the black level alone, for the most part. That makes gain good and brightness bad.

Similarly, contrast does not give you individual control over the blacks and highlights. If you increase contrast, it raises the highlights by the same amount that it lowers setup, or black. The best way to increase contrast is to lower setup and raise gain individually.

Save a Color

When you have eyedroppered a color using the color swatches in the Color Correction Toolset's Color Match Controls, you can save those colors to a Bin. Once they are saved to a bin, you can recall them from the bin and use that color to match another color.

❶ Eyedropper a color using the Color Match Controls in the Color Correction Toolset.

❷ Alt+drag the color swatch (Opt+drag) into a bin.

❸ The color swatch appears in the bin, much like a regular clip. If you are using the standard Correction setting defaults, the color has a cute name, like "Firebrick Red" and its associated RGB color. (We sampled this from color bars.) You can also provide a descriptive name for the color in the bin.

❹ To use this color to match to another color, drag the color back to the right-hand swatch (the output swatch) then use the input color swatch to pick the color from the current monitor that you want to match.

❺ Click Match. The Color Match controls provide results that vary depending on which tab you are in (Controls, Hue Offset or Curves). The results also depend on the options you choose from the Color Match Type menu, which is the small pulldown above the Match Color button.

Give a Hoot! Don't Pollute!

Sometimes, when attempting a color correction that is more of an effect, like a sepia tone, it is very difficult to achieve the look you want because the actual colors from the original video pollute the color that you are trying to create. To avoid this, lower the chroma of your image using the Saturation slider in the Controls tab of the Color Correction Toolset. Sometimes, leaving a little of the original color is nice, and with other images you will want to reduce the Saturation to zero. It will take some experience to know whether you should lower the chroma before or after you attempt to do the correction. The stronger you want the color to be affected, the greater the chance that you will want to do this before you start the correction.

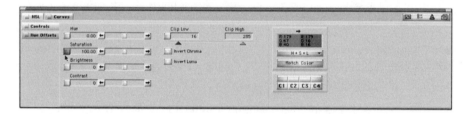

By the Numbers

If you are trying to determine the color casts in the various tonal ranges of your image (shadows, midtones, highlights) you can use the color swatches in the Color Match Controls of the Color Correction Toolset.

- If you sample a color that you believe should be pure white, or pure black, or even a pure shade of gray, then the RGB numbers in the color swatch should all be close to identical.

- If a single color channel dominates the other two, then the color cast is toward that color.

- If one color is lower than the other two, it's a little more complicated: If red is lower than green and blue, then there is a cyan cast. If green is lower than red and blue, then there is a magenta cast, and if blue is lower than red and green, then there is a yellow cast.

Understanding Hue Offsets

The Hue Offset wheels are excellent for fixing color casts. Each wheel represents a different tonal range–shadows, midtones, highlights. If you detect a color cast in one of these tonal ranges it is very simple to eliminate this color cast with the Hue Offset wheels. Whichever direction the color cast goes in one of the tonal ranges, drag the center cursor on the wheel for that range away from the color of the cast. So if you detect a blue cast in the midtones, drag the center of the Midtone wheel away from blue, towards yellow.

If you are unsure of the exact color cast, you can use the eyedroppers below each wheel to sample the color and eliminate the cast automatically.

❶ Open the Color Correction Toolset and the HSL tab and the Hue Offsets subtab.

❷ Select the problem shot in the Timeline so that it is in the current monitor.

❸ Find an area of the shot that you believe is pure white. Click on the eyedropper under the Highlight Hue Offset wheel (the one on the right), then click on the spot that should be white. The color cast is removed.

Color casts in the midranges and shadows can be removed by using the eyedropper under the appropriate Hue Offset wheels. If you don't like the affect it has on the color, you can Alt-click (Opt-click) on the button under the wheel to the left of the eyedropper.

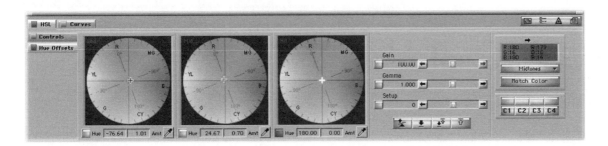

Understanding Curves

Curves is a way to make very fine tonal range adjustments to the RGB levels—and the master level.

The master curve determines levels in a similar way to adjusting the setup, gamma and gain levels, but instead of only having those three tonal ranges to adjust, you can select up to 16 different points on the curve to adjust. This is very helpful if you want to leave the very darkest blacks where they are but move the pretty dark blacks up a bit. You do not have that kind of fine control over specific tonal ranges with sliders.

The R, G, and B curves allow you that same fine level of tonal range control in each of the color channels. The color schemes in each Curves graph represent the color cast that occurs if you drag the curve toward that color. In other words, if you drag the blue curve downward or forward, the cast in that tonal range will become yellow.

To make a correction using Curves, click on a point in the curve. Highlights are represented by the top-right corner of the curve, and shadows are represented by the bottom-left corner. Pick the tonal range you want to affect on the color channel you want to affect, and drag it up or down or forward or back.

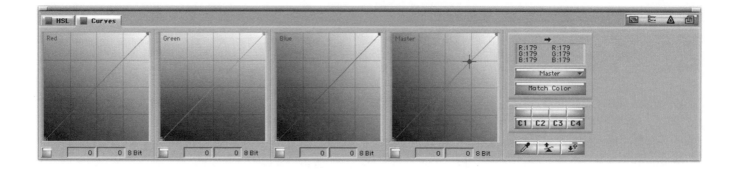

Spot Color Correction

You can do spot color correction–a color correction where the correction is limited to some geographic area of the image–using any matte key and the standard color correction tools. You can create these mattes in Photoshop if you want, or if you're not a big Photoshop geek, you can make them in the Title tool.

❶ Create a circle by dragging the circle tool from one corner of the screen to the other and add a slight shadow to it. Change the fill opacity to 0 and the shadow to white, so you can see it, then soften the shadow to 39.

❷ From the File menu, Export the title. This will create a TIFF file with a soft, circular alpha channel.

❸ Import that file into a bin.

❹ Cut the imported matte onto v2 over the section of the sequence where you want your spot color correction.

❺ Use Mark Clip to mark the matte clip's in and out, but select v1 and copy that exact section of video by using Ctrl+C (Cmd+C).

❻ Step into your matte key using the Step In button and cut the copied video onto the fill track (should be v2) of the matte.

❼ Now if you want the correction to be inside the circle, go into color correction mode on the footage inside the matte. If you want the outside of the circle to have the correction, then go into color correction mode on v1. Or correct both tracks.

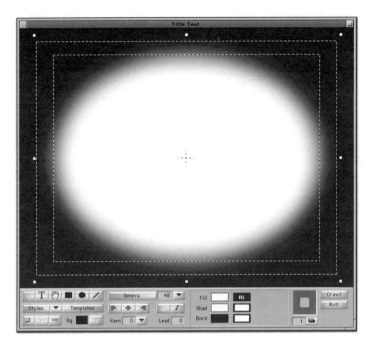

ON THE SPOT

A Few Good Menus

A Grand Entrance

TIX, TOX, TIX, TOX

A Graceful Exit

Loop Dreams

Runnin' Back and Forth

H-Bomb

Man with the MultiCam

An Extended Stay

Sync or Swim

Based on a True Storyboard

Bin and Purge

Analyze This

A Brief Intermission

Trim Cycle

AutoSync or Swim

It's the Same Old Song

CHAPTER 7

Can It Be Faster?

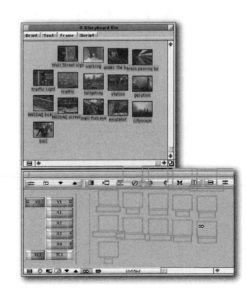

Whether you've been using Avid editing systems for 15 days or 15 years, you will always find newer, faster, and better ways of doing things. (Whoever said that you can't teach an old dog new tricks never met an Avid power user.) In the time-sensitive world of television and film postproduction, every second counts. And these timesaving tips and tricks will help you conserve those precious minutes, hours, and possibly days to help you meet those tight deadlines. Many users are intimidated by the myriad Avid functions, and they may hesitate to endeavor uncharted territories. Hopefully, these tips will explain how to use those mysterious functions to help you improve your efficiency, and achieve "power user" status. Get ready to say to yourself, "I didn't know you could do that."

A Few Good Menus

The Clip Name menu above the source monitor stores the last 20 loaded clips. This is where you can quickly retrieve a recent clip rather than loading it from its bin. So, if you know ahead of time which clips you will need, you can load them first and work with them later. By default, the Clip Name Menu will display the last 20 clips in alphabetical order. But if you hold the Alt or Option key, the Clip Name Menu will display the clips in the reverse order in which they were loaded. The Clip Name Menu above the Record Monitor has the same functionality with recently loaded sequences.

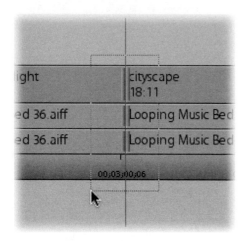

A Grand Entrance

If you've ever wondered why there are so many different ways to do the same thing, it's because each method has its own timesaving advantages. For example, there are a few ways to enter Trim Mode. Clicking the Trim Mode button or pressing the [key will enter Trim Mode for the edit closest to the blue bar position indicator based on your track selection. If no tracks are selected, then the Trim Mode button will select all of the tracks of the closest edit. But what if the edit you want to trim is no where near the blue bar? Regardless of where your blue bar is, you can also enter Trim Mode by lassoing an edit from outside the track area. Certainly you could park the blue bar first, but if you're going to use the mouse anyway, might as well just lasso and save yourself a few seconds. Only the tracks you lasso will be trimmed. If you want to lasso an area within the track area, hold the Alt (or Ctrl) key. Sometimes you have to exit Trim Mode in order to review a large area of your sequence. If you click the Trim Mode button or press the [key while holding the Alt (or Option) key, the Avid will re-enter Trim Mode with your previous roller configuration.

TIX, TOX, TIX, TOX

If your segments are too long in the sequence, you can use a quick keyboard combination to extract their tops or tails; T-I-X and T-O-X. With the appropriate tracks selected, park the blue bar position indicator to the spot where you want to cut.

To extract the top of a segment:

❶ Press T to mark In and Out points at the head and tail frames of the segment.

❷ Press O to mark a new Out point at the blue bar.

❸ Press X to extract the region.

To extract the tail of a segment:

❶ Press T to mark the clip.

❷ Press I to mark a new In point at the blue bar.

❸ Press X to extract the region.

You can easily remember that T-I-X is for tail and T-O-X is for top because the word "tail" has an "I" in it and "top" has an "O." These keys are pretty convenient if you already have your right hand over J-K-L. But if you're a lefty, you may find it easier to use E to Mark In and R to Mark Out, so that you can quickly hit T-E-X and T-R-X with your left hand. (You can even do this with a single button on higher-end Avids, because they have extract Top and Tail as standard editing functions.) Keep in mind that this depends on your track selection, so be careful not to break sync or accidentally extract frames from other tracks.

111

A Graceful Exit

There are a few ways to exit Trim Mode, each with its own timesaving advantage. If you exit Trim Mode by clicking the Trim Mode button or the [key on the keyboard, the Avid will activate the Record Monitor so you can continue to review the sequence from the blue bar. If you exit Trim Mode by hitting the Escape key, Avid will activate the Source Monitor so you can audition the next shot you may want to edit. You can also exit Trim Mode by using the Jog keys 1, 2, 3, and 4, so if you've just finished trimming and you want to back up one second to review your work, press the 1 key three times. Exiting Trim Mode by clicking the timecode track will also move the blue bar to wherever you click, so you can review your sequence from any point in time.

Loop Dreams

While using Trim Mode, a lot of time is wasted by stopping to review your work. Instead, you can trim and review simultaneously. While looping playback, as the blue bar moves, hit I or O to trim the selected side(s) to whichever frame you are seeing during the loop. Or, you can review an edit and simultaneously trim it by small increments with the keyboard. While looping in Trim Mode, press the Trim Buttons M, comma, period, and / to trim the selected side(s) by -10, -1, +1, or +10 respective frames, and the Avid will continue to loop the edit to review your work.

Runnin' Back and Forth

Normally, the Previous and Next Edit buttons are sensitive to your track selection, and they move the blue bar to whichever edits the selected tracks have in common. Many editors find this behavior annoying, since most of the time the only edits the tracks have in common are the very beginning and end of the sequence. So, editors might waste a lot of time selecting and deselecting the appropriate tracks just to get these buttons to behave. There's got to be a better way, right? Just hold the Alt (or Option) key while using the Previous and Next Edit buttons, and the blue bar will move to the closest edit regardless of your track selection. And if you get tired of holding the Alt (or Option) key, you can make the Avid hold it for you by adding the Alt (or Option) key to the button from the Other tab in the Command Palette.

H-Bomb

Have you ever needed to quickly edit a music video or montage so that your cuts occur on the beat? With the Add Edit command, mapped to the H key, you can premap your edits ahead of time.

1. Create a new sequence and edit the music into your audio tracks.

2. Select only the empty video track, play the sequence, and press the H key each time you want a cut to occur. This will create several filler segments in the video tracks that begin and end wherever you press H.

3. Go back and replace each filler segment with a video clip.

Man with the MultiCam

If your source clips are from a multiple-camera shoot and they are synced by either timecode, In points, or Out points, you can quickly edit them by using MultiCam or Group Clip Mode. (This works only in Express Pro.)

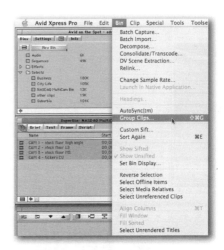

1. Select the synced clips, go to the bin's Fast Menu, and choose Group Clips.

2. Edit the group clip into a sequence.

3. Go to the Special menu to enter Group Clip mode.

4. The Group Clip will appear in a Quad Split view, and although it will not play in real time, you can choose the next shot by clicking on its quadrant.

5. Alternatively, you can map M1-4 from the MCam tab of the Command Palette to your keyboard, and cut to the desired shot by hitting the appropriate key. Once again, you won't see the shots change in real time, so you'll have to stop playback to review your work.

An Extended Stay

If your only Avid experience has been with older versions of Avid Xpress DV, then you should learn about extend edits. Extend edits allow you to quickly perform a double-roller trim without having to enter Trim Mode.

❶ First, clear any In or Out points you may have in the sequence.

❷ Select the track(s) to trim, and park the blue bar position indicator to where you want the new edit.

❸ If you want to extend the A side, mark an Out point. If you want to extend the B side, mark an In point.

❹ Click the Extend button.

Since entering Trim Mode brings the blue bar to the edit, one reason why you may choose to use Extend instead of a double-roller trim is to avoid moving the blue bar.

Sync or Swim

If you need to sync two segments together in a sequence, such as a video action to an audio event, you can use locators to help you slip them into place. Add Locators to the two segments at the point in which they need to be synced. Park the blue bar between the two locators, press Shift+T to mark In and Out points at the locators, and click on the Tracking Information menu above the Record Monitor to see the duration between I/O. This number minus one frame is the exact amount you need to slip the segments in sync.

Based on a True Storyboard

When a bin is in Frame View, you can mark In and Out points in selected clips without the need of the Source or popup monitor. Select the clip, press the 5 key, the spacebar, or J-K-L to play the clip, and press I and O while the clip is playing. If several selected clips are dragged from their bin to the Timeline, they will be spliced into the sequence in the order in which they appear in the bin, a process known as storyboard editing. If you want to overwrite the clips instead of splicing them in, enter red Segment Mode first.

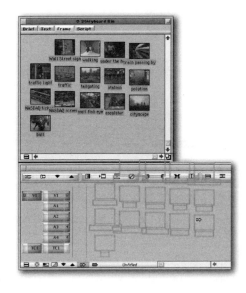

Bin and Purge

Whenever you launch an existing project, the Avid will also automatically launch all of the bins that were left open during the last time you worked on that project. If these recently opened bins contain long sequences, then you may have to wait a long time for the Avid to finish loading all of the bins before you can continue to work. However, if you hold the Alt (or Option) key while you click OK to open the project, the Avid will not open any of these recent bins, and you can begin working right away.

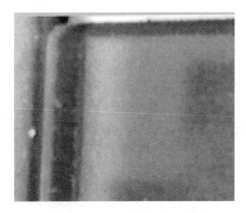

Analyze This

When you are cutting clips with sound on tape, particularly with dialogue footage, you may encounter edits where you have obvious changes in audio level or room tone because of each shot's different microphone setup. If you need to trim in these kinds of situations, you may find it difficult to figure out if you need to trim the A side or the B side. So, what do you do? In Trim Mode, you can analyze each side of the edit to help you isolate the problem. While looping playback in Trim Mode, press Q to loop only the A side or W to loop only the B side of the edit. Once you've determined the appropriate side, select it, and trim away.

A Brief Intermission

If your pre-roll and post-roll settings are somewhat short, then looping playback in Trim Mode may happen too quickly. Or, when Trim Mode begins to loop again, the switch from the B side to the A side may cause confusion by appearing to be an edit. To avoid these situations, set up a trim intermission. In the Settings tab of the Project window, double-click the Trim settings, and give yourself a few seconds of intermission. The Avid will now pause before it begins looping again, giving you precious seconds to think about the edit, or just enjoy a moment of silence.

Trim Cycle

In Trim Mode, a quick way to choose which side to trim is to use the Cycle Trim Sides button. From the Trim tab of the Command Palette, map the Cycle Trim Sides button to the keyboard, perhaps to the U key. Then in Trim Mode, you can toggle your rollers to trim either the A side, B side, or both. You can also use this button in Source/Record Modes to toggle between the Source and Record Monitors in the Composer window.

AutoSync or Swim

Once in a while, you may record audio separate from video, or you may need to add a piece of audio to a video clip. the Avid can create a synced clip for you. This is often done with film, since audio is acquired separately.

❶ Load your video in the Source Monitor and place an In point at a specific frame. With film, this is most often the frame when the clappers hit.

❷ Load your audio in the Source Monitor and place an In point at the same specific moment. Once again with film, this is most often the frame when the clappers hit. (Hint: Click the Toggle Source/Record in Timeline button to see the audio sample plot of a clip in the Source Monitor.)

❸ Select both clips in their bin, go to the Bin menu, choose AutoSync(tm), and use Inpoints. You now have a new ".sync" clip with video and audio.

It's the Same Old Song

Want to avoid choosing a user and project each time you launch the Avid? There is a setting that instructs the system to automatically open the most recent project with the most recent user profile. In the Settings tab of the Project window, double-click the active Interface setting–the one with the check mark next to it. From the General tab, choose Automatically Launch Last Project at Startup.

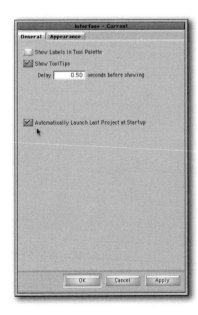

ON THE SPOT

A Cut Above

Transition effects are more than just dissolves, wipes, and page peels. How you choose to transition from one shot to another influences how both shots are interpreted in the context of your show. But, that's enough theory from Filmmaking 101. Leave the cultural, historical, and sociopolitical media analysis to someone else. This chapter will teach you several tricks for building custom transition effects. Whether you are editing weddings, corporate videos, children's programming, or DVD menus, your clients may be expecting to see more than the standard iris or shape wipes. Learn how to spice it up to be a cut above the rest. If a picture is worth a thousand words, then how you go from one image to another can say volumes in establishing your style and setting the overall mood of your show.

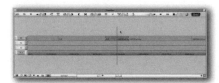

Segments in Transition

By default, several segment effects cannot be applied as transitions. However, with a little nesting trick, any segment effect can appear to be a transition.

① Using the Add Edit command (mapped as the H key by default), add equidistant edits on either side of a cut.

② Select the two new adjacent segments in Segment Mode, hold Alt (or Option), and double-click the desired segment effect in the Effect Palette. The two adjacent segments will automatically nest together, and the effect will be applied to the nest.

③ Symmetrical keyframing will make the segment effect look like a transition. You only need a few minutes of experimentation with each effect to see which ones you will like best. A few examples will be highlighted in this chapter.

Flip Flop and Fly

The 3D flip transition may seem like a relic from television's past, but it's still used in news and children's programming. While several variations of this effect are included with a number of effects packages, knowing how to build it from scratch allows you to control each of its parameters, such as drop shadow, background image, and rotation angle.

① With the H key, add equidistant edits on either side of a cut.

② Enter Segment Mode, and select the two new adjacent segments.

③ Hold Alt (or Option), and double-click the 3D PIP from the Blend category of the Effect Palette.

④ Enable Shadow, and crop any video blanking on the edges of the frame.

⑤ Keyframe either X, Y, or Z rotation from 0 to 180.

⑥ Depending on which axis rotates, the B side may appear flipped or flopped. Step into the effect and apply to the B side a Flip, Flop, or Flip-Flop to fix the transition.

Camera Flash

The camera flash transition is one we see a lot in trailers for horror or science fiction movies. It looks similar to a white dip to color, except the images appear to wash out as if they were overexposed, or brightened by a flash bulb.

❶ With the H key, add equidistant edits on either side of a cut.

❷ Enter Segment Mode and select the two new adjacent segments.

❸ Hold Alt (or Option), and double-click the Color Effect from the Image category of the Effect Palette.

❹ With both keyframes of the Color Effect selected, make sure the Luma Range White Point is set to 235. This is the brightest white acceptable for broadcast.

❺ In the middle of the effect, create a keyframe, and set the Luma Range White Point to 16. This is the darkest black acceptable for broadcast.

Adjusting the timing of the flash will create different feelings. So, if the segments have enough handle, experiment by Alt- or Option-dragging the middle keyframe to move it, step into the nest, and use a double-roller to trim the edit to the same position of the middle keyframe.

Also, if you are working on a higher-end Avid, you can also keyframe a defocus to emphasize the look of the flash.

Wipe On, Wipe Off

While there are plenty of wipe effects in the Edge Wipe category, they each have a fixed angle. If you want an edge wipe with a different angle, you can combine a Matte Key with a 3D Page Fold to achieve the same look.

❶ Using two video tracks, overlap the beginning of the B shot over the end of the A shot.

❷ In a third empty video track, add edits in the filler above the overlap.

❸ Apply a 3D Page Fold onto the filler segment, set its Shape Radius to 0, its Shape Angle to whichever degree you prefer, and in the Foreground parameter group, turn on Reverse Animation and Show Alpha. You should see a black screen wipe onto a white one.

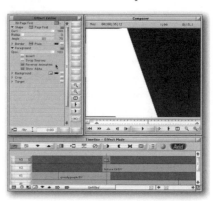

❹ Now, hold Alt (or Option), and apply a Matte Key onto the same filler segment.

Wipe On, Wipe Off (with Graphic)

The graphic edge wipe is used a lot in broadcasts for live sporting events, entertainment news, promotional corporate videos, weddings, graduations, and DVD menu or track transitions.

❶ Start with the custom edge wipe described above.

❷ Edit a graphic with an alpha channel into a higher track directly above the filler segment.

❸ Promote the graphic Matte Key to 3D to make it easier to animate across the screen.

❹ Using the head and tail keyframes, create a straight motion path to animate the graphic from one side of the screen to the other.

❺ Adjust the timing of the 3D Page Fold underneath to match the graphic's animation.

Crooked Wipe On, Wipe Off

Want to create your own wipe with any possible edge?

❶ Create an oversized grayscale image in a graphics application, such as Adobe Photoshop.

❷ Using two video tracks, overlap the beginning of the B shot over the end of the A shot.

❸ In a third empty video track, add edits in the filler above the overlap.

❹ Apply Avid Pan & Zoom onto the filler segment, and click on the Other Options button in the upper left of the Effect Editor to import the oversized graphic.

❺ Animate the graphic's position to create the transition.

❻ Now, hold Alt (or Option), and apply a Matte Key onto the same filler segment.

Luck of the Iris

Custom iris transitions are frequently seen in weddings, corporate videos, and children's programming; they are usually in the shape of a heart, star, or company logo.

❶ With a graphics application such as Adobe Photoshop, create a image with a black shape on a white background.

❷ Using two video tracks, overlap the beginning of the B shot over the end of the A shot.

❸ Edit the black and white graphic into a higher track directly above the overlap.

❹ Apply a Matte Key onto the graphic segment.

❺ Step into the Matte Key and apply a 3D PIP.

❻ Set the 3D PIP's Background Luminance to 255, and animate Scaling to create the iris wipe. You may need to adjust the 3D PIP's Crop settings to remove any video blanking.

Templates to That Effect

If you've spent a good chunk of your precious time creating a transition effect, why not save it so you can apply it elsewhere? With a transition open in the Effect Editor, save it by dragging its icon into a bin. You may want to create a separate bin for transitions and another bin for segment effects. Keyframes are also saved with the template. If you have a saved effect that has the same parameter group as another effect, you can apply the saved parameters onto the current effect by dropping onto the appropriate group in the Effect Editor. The borrowed parameters will be applied only to selected keyframes.

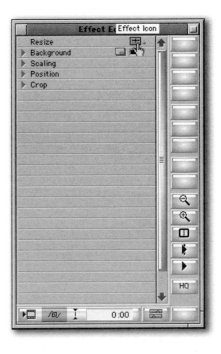

Plasma TV

When you register Avid Xpress Pro or DV, you receive the activation codes to install PlasmaWipes. These are effects that are driven by grayscale images. While the installation includes several pre-made images, you can use Adobe Photoshop to make your own.

❶ For NTSC, create gradient images at 720×486 pixels. For PAL, use 720×576.

❷ Save your images in the Photoshop Raw format and make sure they have the .raw file extension.

❸ While the Avid is not running, place these files in the proper location in the SupportingFiles folder.

If you're not very good at drawing your own gradient images, there are plenty of places where you can download some free. Just make sure they are the correct frame size and save them in the .raw format.

Plasma Laboratory

Here are a couple of tips for designing your own PlasmaWipe images. Draw a full-screen gradient with the Gradient tool, and experiment with different Distort filters for a myriad of possibilities. For brush or paint stroke transitions, use a large Brush or Pencil with its "Other Dynamics" set to a large Fade Opacity.

Tweak a Dissolve

Sometimes when you are adding dissolves, you can play with the duration or placement of the dissolve and never get a transition that feels entirely smooth. Sometimes, the solution is to get away from the standard linear dissolves and use a film dissolve.

Film dissolves are made to simulate the look of an optical film dissolve instead of an electronic dissolve, so they react differently.

Park on a transition and press the \ key, which is the default button for Quick Transition. From the Dissolve pulldown menu, choose Film Dissolve. Film Dissolves are also accessible from the Effects Palette in the Film category.

In addition to the difference in the look of the film dissolve you can also choose to alter the Acceleration of the effect, which makes the beginning and end of the effect slower and the middle of the effect faster. (You can also change the Acceleration on regular dissolves.)

Super Zoom

Made popular by *CSI: Crime Scene Investigation*, the super zoom transition is now being used a lot in product shots and movie trailers. Here's how to make it.

1 Edit two clips together. To make the super zoom effect look more convincing, the first should be a wide shot, and the second should be a close up of the same subject.

2 About 10 frames before the cut, click the Add Edit button to cut the last few frames of the wide shot.

3 Apply a Resize (from the Image category) to this segment, and animate its scale and position to match its tail frame with the first frame of the close-up.

4 On this same segment, Alt-drag (Option-drag) a Radial Blur (from the Illusion FX category).

5 Set the Radial Blur's Zoom setting to something like 7.0, its Angle to 0, and its Render Quality to High.

6 Animate the center of the Radial Blur to focus on your subject.

Ripple Study

Typically used to transition between "before" and "after" shots, the ripple dissolve is commonly seen in commercials and promotional videos.

1 Apply a Dissolve between two segments in the sequence.

2 With the H key, add equidistant edits on either side of a cut.

3 Enter Segment Mode and select the two new adjacent segments.

4 Hold Alt (or Option), and double-click the Ripple from the Illusion FX category of the Effect Palette.

5 Adjust the border parameters to remove the video blanking on the edges of the image.

6 Adjust the many parameters to customize the look of the ripple(s).

7 Keyframe Amount from 0 to 100.

Dream a Little Dream of Me

Typically used to transition a dream sequence, the wave dissolve is commonly seen as a stylistic element in popular sitcoms and dramas.

❶ Apply a Dissolve between two segments in the sequence.

❷ With the H key, add equidistant edits on either side of a cut.

❸ Enter Segment Mode and select the two new adjacent segments.

❹ Hold Alt (or Option), and double-click the Wave from the Illusion FX category of the Effect palette.

❺ Adjust the Border parameters to remove the video blanking on the edges of the image.

❻ Adjust the many Input Parameters to customize the look of the waves.

❼ Keyframe Amount from 0 to 100 and back to 0.

Fade Effect

Whenever you need to create a transition for a segment effect, a quick way is to use the Fade Effect button. This works with any effect that has a Foreground parameter, including titles, and automatically sets keyframes based on how much you want to Fade Up and Fade Down. This is much more efficient than using Dissolves on either side of the segment because you would only need to render one effect instead of three.

SWISH!

Wish they'd shot some swish pans for a high-energy sequence you're trying to cut together? Fake 'em! Swish pans look best when used for short durations. 4-7 frames is usually about right.

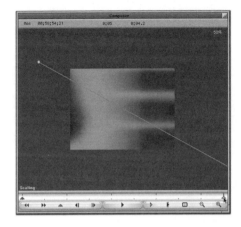

❶ Add an edit 4 to 7 frames before your current cut.

❷ Drop a 3D PIP on the small segment.

❸ Resize the segment to 400 percent or larger, which can be done by using both Scale and Target.

❹ Adjust the Position of the first keyframe to one side of the large PIP and the last frame to the other side. Voila! You've got a swish pan.

Effect on Filler

One excellent way to do transitions is to add them to filler *above* the actual video track where you would normally apply them. This way you can change the video underneath without having to step into it. You can actually put multiple layers of effects on tracks above your video track, and they will all be applied to the track below.

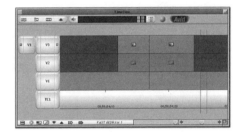

An excellent use of this tip is to combine it with the tip about creating an organic-feeling "camera flash" that is described earlier in this chapter.

❶ About four frames before your cut on V1, do an Add Edit in the filler to video tracks 2 and 3. Add another set of Add Edits in the filler directly above the cut and a third set of Add Edits about 6 or 7 frames after the edit on V1. This creates two small segments of filler between the Add Edits on video tracks 2 and 3.

❷ In each small section of filler on track 2, drop the color effect as described in the Camera Flash tip.

❸ In the small sections of filler on track 3, add a blur effect from either the Illusion FX or from a third-party AVX effect. Start the blur at 0 and ramp it up as it approaches the cut point on V1 then on the filler after the edit, start the blur where the other blur left off and ramp it back to 0.

❹ Now you can change the video on V1 as many times as you want without having to redo the effects. (You will have to re-render of course.)

ON THE SPOT

CHAPTER 9

Notching It Up

Sometimes what is shot is not enough. Sometimes a cut is not the right transition. Sometimes there isn't quite enough in the tape bin to tell your story. That is when you press Ctrl+8 (Cmd+8) to call in the heavy artillery: effects.

Effects add sizzle. They can help explain and sell. Effects are the icing on the cake.

Whether you are just looking to add a novel transition or you're going to hit your video with every single effect in the palette, there are things you can do to make your life easier and get you to the effect you want faster. This chapter will show you how to deliver big, yet make it all look and feel effortless.

If You'd Rather Forget It: Reset It

Sometimes if an adjustment to a parameter just isn't working, you want to get back to square one and start fresh. The easiest way to do that for a single parameter is to Alt (Option) click on the effect parameter's "enable" button.

A straight click on this button will toggle the effect parameter from enabled to disabled, but the parameters that are set within the pane remain where they were left.

Get a Promotion

One of the most common effects mistakes is trying to add a 3D move to a title or an alpha matte key. If you drop a 3D effect on one of these effects, any move you make will not only affect the foreground (title) but also the background (your video)!

The correct way to add a move to a title or alpha matte key (like a graphic with an alpha channel from Photoshop) is to promote the title to 3D.

❶ Cut your title or key onto V2 of your sequence above your video on V1.

❷ Go into Effect Mode by clicking on the Effect Mode icon or using the keyboard shortcut Ctrl+8 (Cmd+8).

❸ At the bottom-right corner of the title or matte key Effect Editor is a small button that looks like a wireframe drawing of a cube. Click on that.

That promotes the effect to 3D and adds almost a dozen new effects parameters to your Effect Editor. You can move your effect in 3D space this way without taking the background video along for the ride.

Smooth Move

When doing 3D moves you may feel that the effect either jerks as it starts or slams to a stop at the end. If you would like to ease in or ease out of these moves, in the Effect Editor on many effects is a parameter called Acceleration.

Twirl down the parameter's right-pointing triangle to reveal the parameter slider. The default for Acceleration is 0. This means that the move will be linear, which means that its speed is constant from beginning to end. Linear motion is completely unnatural. Natural motion begins slowly and ends slowly and is quicker in the middle. Moving the slider to 100 provides the highest level of ease in and ease out. Start with 100 and see if you want to adjust it from there.

Just a Skosh, Please!

OK, we all need a "skosh" button, right? Producers and directors are always looking for just that practically imperceptible move from what you already did that will make it perfect. Well, rest easy, mate! There is a "skosh" button on your keyboard.

Whenever you need to move an effect the smallest possible amount (and this works in the Title Tool as well) you can use your arrow keys.

- In the Effect Editor, you need to have clicked on a specific effects parameter slider to use the right and left arrow keys. If you attempt to move the effect in the Effect Monitor with the arrow keys, you will simply move through the effect in the Timeline one frame at a time.

- In the Title Tool, you can select a text box or other element and move it on the screen using any of the arrow keys.

Constrain Yourself!

In the Effects Mode and in the Title Tool, when you are moving elements, you can constrain the movement of the mouse to purely vertical or horizontal movement by holding down the Shift key before you begin to drag. This is an excellent way to draw straight lines with the Title Tool's Line Tool.

Shift-dragging also works with the Title Tool drawing tools to constrain the Rectangle Tool to a perfect square and to constrain the Oval Tool to a perfect circle. This is a fairly common keyboard shortcut that works similarly in many programs.

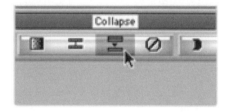

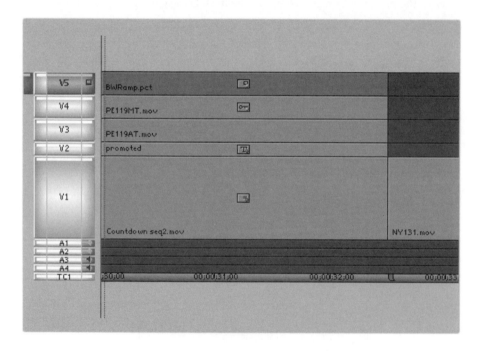

Saving Private Effects

Many effects that you use today, you will reuse tomorrow. There is nothing that makes doing effects faster than a little recycling. Even if you are not going to reuse the effect exactly as it was used before, it's still usually faster to start with something similar than it is to start from scratch.

Start an effects bin and open it every time you start a new project. Each time you come up with a cool effect, either drag the effect to this new bin or subclip the section in the sequence and put the subclip in the bin. You can always step in to an effect and replace the video within.

Kill the Source but Spare the Effect

Let's say you promoted a title to 3D and created a cool move on it. Now you want to use that move for all of the titles in a show but you don't want to have to recreate it. Here's what you do:

❶ With the Timeline locator on the title and the title's video track selected, go into effect mode. This calls up the promoted title effect in the Effect Editor.

❷ Alt+drag (Option+drag) the title effect (small purple T) from the top of the Effect Editor into a bin.

❸ In the bin, this clip will be labeled 3D Title: promoted (without source). If you had simply dragged the clip into the bin, it would have taken the source (the text) along with it.

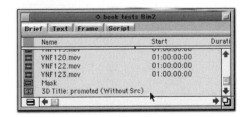

Now, all you have to do to apply the 3D move to any other title is drag the effect from the bin onto a title in the Timeline. This trick also works for matte keys with alpha channels, like graphics brought in from Photoshop.

Fade to Black

One of the fastest ways to make your effects look bad is to make the transitions in to and out of them look bad. Here are some tips for transitioning to or from an effects stack.

For transitions at the beginning or end of a sequence where you want to fade from black or fade to black, using dissolves as you would on a single video layer will not create a clean transition. If you put a dissolve on each layer of the effect stack, the effects will become transparent at the same time they're fading to black. You can fix this with one simple effect:

❶   Select the top layer of your effects stack and press the \ key which, on the default keyboard is Quick Transition.

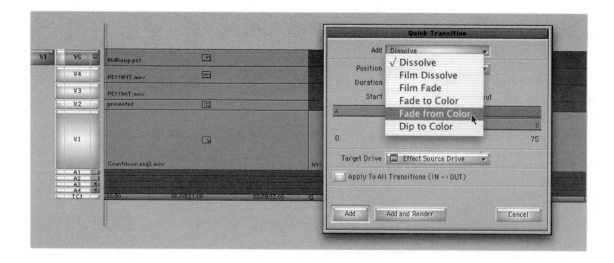

❷   At the top of the Quick Transition window is a button that usually reads Dissolve. Click on this to reveal a pulldown window.

❸   Select Fade From Color to fade up or choose Fade To Color to fade to black. The default color is black so there's no need to do anything else except set the duration.

The Fade From Color on only the top layer will create a clean transition for all of the effects in the layer.

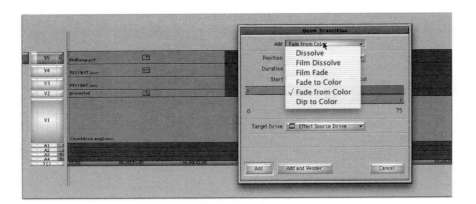

Be the Submaster of Your Domain

When trying to dissolve from one stack of effects to another stack, or from a stack to a single track of video, the easiest way to create a clean transition is to submaster the stack.

Select all of the tracks in the stack and mark an in at the beginning of the stack and an out at the end. Make sure that you don't accidentally mark the first frame of the next stack! (You can also just submaster the last second or so of the effects stack, but this makes it very hard to do revisions later.)

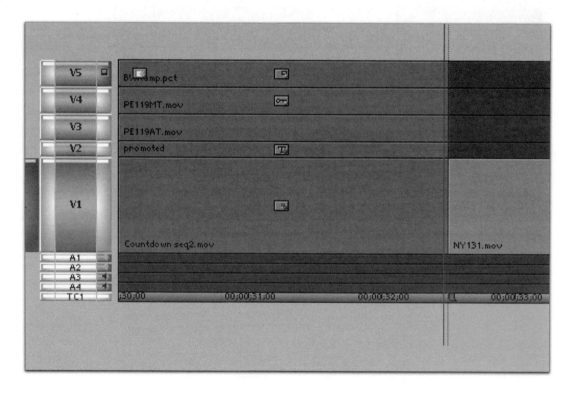

Click on the Collapse button in the Timeline toolbar or wherever else you may have this button mapped. This will Collapse the effect stack into a single video track.

Now you can transition in and out of this single track in any way you want. This is much easier to handle. If you later need to change shots in the submaster, you can either double click on the submaster effect in Effect Mode to expand it or you can use the Step In and Step Out buttons–the two small, black up and down arrows–at the bottom of the Timeline to be able to look into and edit the segments in the submaster.

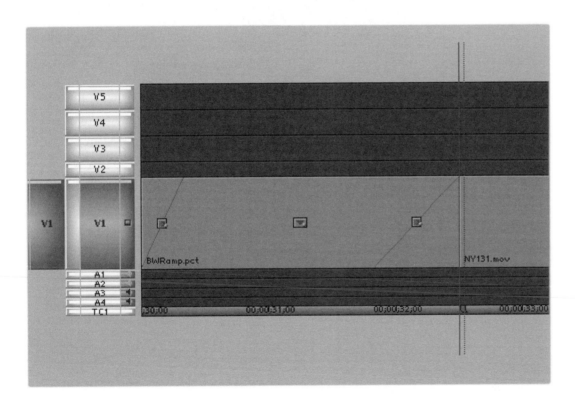

A Soft Anchor

Sometimes when creating titles, it is difficult to make the title stand out against a busy video background. One of the subtlest ways to improve legibility is to create a soft anchor for the text. But with no way to make soft boxes, how can you do it?

❶ Open the Title Tool by choosing Clip>New Title and create your text.

❷ With the Rectangle Tool, create a rectangle that completely covers your text.

3 Change the opacity of the Fill of the rectangle to 0.

4 From the menus at the top of Xpress Pro, choose Object>Send Backwards.

5 Add a slight drop shadow to the rectangle and lower the opacity so that the text pops nicely but some of the video shows through as well.

6 From the menus at the top of Xpress Pro again, choose Object>Soften Shadow. In the Soft Shadow box, start with a 20-pixel blur. You may want to go all the way up to 40 or down to 4. Pick something that helps the text pop but doesn't call attention to itself with hard edges.

Fill 'Er Up!

You can fill a title with video or any texture or color that you have in a bin.

❶ Create a title in the Title Tool. It must use video as a background. It is also wise not to have a drop shadow, because the video will fill anyplace with an alpha key and it can't distinguish between the face of the font and the drop shadow. This effect works best with large, fat fonts.

❷ Edit your title into your sequence.

❸ Step in to the title by parking the Timeline locator on the title and clicking on the Step In button, which is the small, black, downward-pointing triangle in the bottom left of your Timeline. Now the Timeline only shows the inside of the Title Tool effect, with a locked alpha channel on V3, the fill on V2, and nothing on V1.

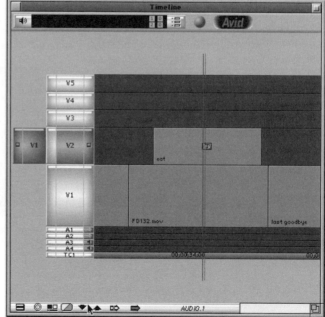

image courtesy of ArtBeats' – Food 1 Collection

④ Call up the footage you want to fill the letters in the Source Monitor.

⑤ Patch your source to V2 on the sequence side and Mark Clip, to place edits at both ends of the fill track. Hit the "B" button on the default keyboard to overwrite the original fill on V2 with your source footage.

⑥ Step out of the title by clicking on the Step Out button, which is the small, black, upward-pointing triangle in the bottom left of your Timeline.

⑦ Play the effect back.

You can use anything for the fill track. You can even put transitions like wipes inside between two different shots.

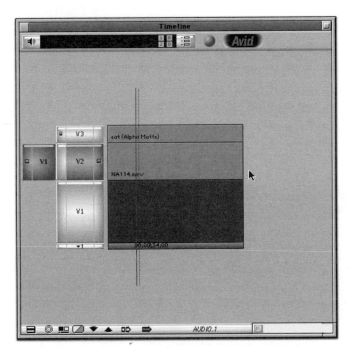

One Effect for All and All Effects from One!

It's quick and easy to drop the same effect on multiple segments or multiple transitions.

❶ The first thing to do is to apply the effect to a single segment or transition and customize it.

❷ Save the effect to a bin by dragging the small effect icon in the upper-right corner of the Effect Editor into a bin. You can name this effect just as you would a regular clip.

❸ In Effect Mode, select multiple segments or transitions by Shift-selecting them. You may need to use Segment Mode to select segments. If you want most or all of your sequence, you can also lasso the segments you want. (It is possible to do this without being in Effect Mode if you are able to select the proper type of effect that you want–transition or segment.)

❹ Double-click the effect in the bin, and it will be applied to all selected segments.

You can also choose effects straight out of the Effect Palette, but this will apply a non-customized effect obviously. You may also experience a "wrong format" bug sometimes if you attempt to apply the effect straight from the Effect Editor without putting it in a bin first.

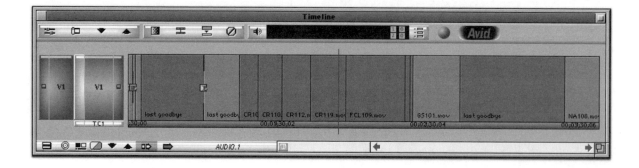

Effect a Single Parameter

If you have saved an effect, you can apply that effect to a single parameter of another effect. You can even do this so that a saved title effect applies its parameter to a single parameter of a matte key effect, for example.

❶ With an effect already saved to a bin (See "Kill the Source but Spare the Effect" earlier in this chapter), go into Effects Mode on the effect in the Timeline where you wish to apply the effect. This will call up the Effect Editor on your effect.

❷ Open the parameter in the effect to which you want to apply your saved effect. If you don't see the parameter, you may need to promote the effect to 3D first.

❸ Now, drag the effect from the bin directly into the parameter in the Effect Editor instead of to the effect in the Timeline. This applies the effect so that it only affects that one parameter.

Load It Up!

You may have tried to drop multiple effects on a single segment only to find yourself faced with an uncooperative dialog box, refusing to accommodate your creative ambitions or with your original effect replaced. Don't quit! Put up a fight!

After a single effect has been added to a segment, you need to Alt+drag (Option+drag) any additional effects onto the segment to get them to stick.

A word of caution. It *does* matter the order in which the effects are applied. For example, if you first drop an effect on something to spin it, then another effect to crop it, the crop happens *after* the spin, thereby cutting off the corners of the effect. Doing it the other way around crops the effect first and then spins the cropped effect.

To access the multiple layers of effects, you use the Step In and Step Out buttons.

Faux Motion Tracker

While Avid Xpress Pro does not include a motion tracker, you can fake it by combining a Flip-Flop, a Resize, and a Region Stabilize. This can be particularly useful if you need to highlight, spot-shadow, or mosiac a face in a crowd.

❶ Edit the same clip three times on top of itself in V1, V2, and V3.

❷ From the Image category, apply Flip-Flop onto the V3 clip.

❸ Alt+ or Option+drag a Resize onto the same clip, and crop it to isolate the area you want to track.

❹ Adjust Position to move that area near the edge of the screen.

❺ On V4, edit a title or graphic to use as a matte, and position it in the opposite side of the screen.

6   Collapse the V3 and V4 tracks, apply Region Stabilize, make sure you are on the first frame of the effect, and select the tracking region.

7   Alt+ or Option+drag a Resize. We'll come back to this to adjust the position of the matte.

8   Alt+ or Option+drag a Matte Key onto the same segment.

9   For a mosaic-type look, apply a Crystal effect (from the Illusion FX category) onto the V1 clip. You should now see that the matte is isolating the Crystal effect. Now, you just need to reposition the matte.

10   In order to see the Crystal effect while adjusting the matte's position, Alt+ or Option+Step In to expand the effect tracks. You should see the previous Resize effect in the 1.3 track.

11   Make sure the 1.3 track is the only one selected, open the Effect Editor, and reposition the matte so that the Crystal effect is covering the tracking area.

ON THE SPOT

CHAPTER 10

Text Is Your Friend

If the pen is mightier than the sword, then the Avid Title Tool puts an entire armory at your disposal. Combine the Avid Title Tool with Adobe Photoshop, and you can take over the world. People who criticize the Avid Title Tool don't realize its full potential. (Plus, it's still a lot better than the built-in title tools of other non-linear video editors.) Quit complaining, and read this chapter! Here, we will teach you several tricks for making professional-looking titles and text effects. Discover valuable shortcuts for saving and applying title styles and templates. See how combining different Avid Xpress Pro effects can bring a new dimension to your text. Learn how to combine techniques in Adobe Photoshop to make those titles leap off of the screen.

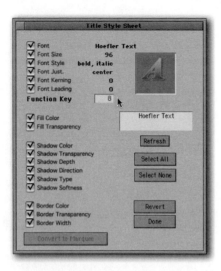

I Like Your Style

Often you need to create several titles with the same format, such as font, size, color, position, etc. To save a title template, click on the Templates button and choose Save Template. If you need to use the template, create a new title, click on the Templates button, and choose Include Template. If you only need to save the style of a piece of text, select it, click the Styles button, choose Save Style, and pick the text attributes you want to save. If you need to take your templates to another system, title templates are saved in the Avid Xpress Pro or DV Settings folder where the application is installed. Title styles are saved with your Avid User settings.

Big Text to Fill

If you want to create a text effect that looks like the letters are magnifying a video clip:

❶   Edit a title over some video.

❷   Step into the title and replace the Graphic Fill with the same video clip as the one below.

❸   While you're still stepped in, apply a Resize onto the new video fill below the alpha matte, and set its scaling to something larger than 100.

❹   Step out, and the text appears to magnify the video, but it may be difficult to read.

❺   To better emphasize the text, promote the title to 3D, and adjust its shadow settings.

Under Lock and Key

Graphics created in the Title Tool have locked alpha mattes that cannot be animated. If you want to animate the matte and you don't have it as a separate graphic, you can copy it from the title, and apply it with a matte key instead.

❶ Step into the title, and replace the Graphic Fill with a video clip.

❷ Select only the alpha matte track, and click Mark Clip to mark In and Out points around the entire matte.

❸ In Source or Record Mode, hold the Alt (Option) key, and press C to copy the alpha matte and load it into the Source Monitor.

❹ Step out of the title, and click Remove Effect to leave the video fill behind.

❺ Edit the alpha matte from the Source Monitor to a track above the video fill, and apply a matte key to it.

❻ If desired, promote the matte key to 3D, and adjust its shadow.

❼ Step into the matte key effect, apply a 3D PIP onto the alpha matte inside, set the 3D PIP's Background Luminance to 255, and animate it however you wish.

❽ You may need to adjust the 3D PIP's crop settings to remove any video blanking.

Wiggle It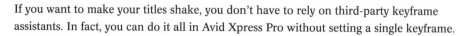

If you want to make your titles shake, you don't have to rely on third-party keyframe assistants. In fact, you can do it all in Avid Xpress Pro without setting a single keyframe.

❶ Edit some shaky, handheld video onto V1 and crop it to isolate a shaky area.

❷ Move that shaky area near the edge of the screen.

❸ On V2, edit a title or graphic, and position it in the cropped area on the opposite side of the screen.

❹ Collapse the tracks, apply Region Stabilize, and select the shaky region.

❺ Alt+ or Option+drag a position effect, such as Resize or PIP, to reposition the video and hide the shaky region.

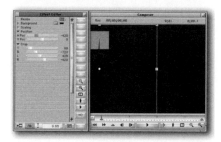

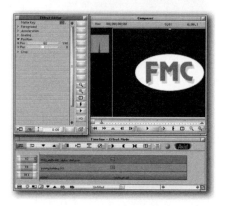

Text Takes Shape

While some of the 3D shape effects may appear to be relics from television's past or the obsessions of a video amateur, these effects can greatly enhance the animation of a graphic or piece of text. Promote a title to 3D, and experiment with what you can do by wrapping the title around a shape. A Page Fold can be used to create a revealing curl animation. With a Ball, you can create an animated sphere effect to make the text or graphic open up from a globe. Also, you can use Slats to create a slant-line scan reveal effect, which is commonly used in news and sports.

A Rolling Title in a Galaxy Far, Far Away

Have you ever wanted to create a Star Wars-style rolling title? With a little help from the Title Tool and the 3D PIP, now you can.

1. In the Title Tool, create a Rolling Title, and edit it into the V1 track.

2. In the empty filler in the V2 track, add edits at the head and tail of the rolling title segment.

3. Apply a 3D PIP to the filler segment.

4. Turn on its black background, turn off its scaling, set its X rotation to something like 60, and its Y position to something like -120.

5. A similar technique on higher-end Avid systems allows you to adjust Corner Pin and Perspective so that the rolling title looks more like it's approaching a vanishing point. But, depending on how you use it, Avid Xpress Pro's 3D PIP may be all you need.

Scroll Control

By default, the rolling and crawling titles move from start to finish based on their durations in the sequence. But in some cases, as with end credits, you may want a rolling title to hold for a few seconds at different places in the text.

❶ Open the title's parameters in the Effect Editor.

❷ First, you can adjust Acceleration to make the motion ease in and out.

❸ When you select the title's start and end keyframes in the Record Monitor, you'll notice that the value for Scroll Position changes. This value indicates where the title enters and exits the screen.

❹ In the Record Monitor, park the blue bar position indicator to whenever you want the title to hold, create a keyframe (N by default), and adjust the Scroll Position slider until you see the title at its holding position.

❺ Move the blue bar forward to when you want the title to resume moving, create another keyframe, and set the Scroll Position to the same value.

❻ If necessary, adjust the positions of the keyframes by Alt+ or Option+dragging them in the Record Monitor. If you need to adjust the duration of the title, no problem. Trimming a title does not affect its text.

❼ Repeat this keyframing process for each time you want the title to hold. If necessary, modify the title so that you have enough blank space between each screen page of text.

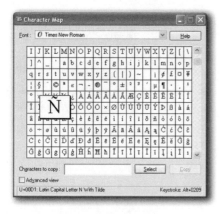

You Are That Special One

In the Title Tool, how the heck do you type those special characters, like © ® ™ £ ¥ ¿ ¡ é ñ and ç? You do it by using a key code that involves holding down the Alt or Option key.

To see key codes on Windows XP:

❶ Go to Start Menu>All Programs>Accessories>System Tools>Character Map.

❷ Select a font and click on a character. Its key code is displayed in the lower-left corner.

❸ For example, to type a ™ symbol, press Alt and type 0153 on the numeric keypad.

To see key codes on Mac OS X:

❶ In Mac OS 10.2, go to Macintosh HD>Applications>Utilities>Key Caps. In Mac OS 10.3, Key Caps is no longer an application but rather a menu item that can be enabled from the Input Menu of the International settings in System Preferences, called Keyboard Viewer.

❷ Select a font, and hold Option or Option+Shift to reveal the special characters.

❸ For example, in order to type a © symbol, press Option+G.

This is particularly useful if you want smart quotes rather than straight quotes or if you need mathematical symbols or characters from other languages. And if you select graphic fonts like Symbol, Dingbat, Webdings, or Wingdings, then you'll most definitely find something you'll ©.

Copy Cat

Many people forget that they can copy text from a word processor and paste it into the Title Tool. Why waste time retyping pages of text when it's already typed somewhere else? And most importantly, if the text originates from a word processor, then you can check if for spelling first. (If your word processor doesn't have a spell checker, then it's time you bite the bullet and spend that extra $150+ for the right tools to do the job right. Heck, you've already got an Avid...) While the Title Tool will not maintain your text formatting from the word processor, it will remember all of your fonts.

Making the Gradient

In the Title Tool, using opacity gradients as backdrops for text can give your title that professional-quality look you see on the news and talk shows.

❶ Begin with the Square and Rectangle Tool, and draw a shape on the screen. For a lower third backdrop, you will definitely want to position it towards the bottom of the screen. Depending on the size of your rectangle, the options in the Alignment menu may save you some time.

❷ With the object selected, you can round the corners of the rectangle by adjusting the Box Corner button at the lower left of the Title Tool.

❸ Click to select the Fill Transparency Selection box, the top-left box of the two rows of swatches near Fill, Shad (shadow), and Bord (border).

❹ To the right of this box are two other boxes that set the opacity levels for the start and end of the gradient. Click and hold one of these boxes, and set it to 100 transparent.

❺ If you don't add any text to this page and edit this gradient into its own track, you can optionally step into the gradient, and replace its Graphic Fill with a clip of a video texture. The gradient's opacity will be maintained, and the lower third text can be added to the track above.

Fruits of My 7 Layers

If you prefer to use Adobe Photoshop 7 to create your text or graphics, you may find it advantageous to draw the different elements on separate layers. Layers in Photoshop documents can be quickly imported as separate tracks, which can in turn, be animated independently. If you use Adobe Photoshop 7 or earlier for NTSC, Avid recommends using a 648×486 frame size for Avid Xpress Pro and 640×480 for Avid Xpress DV. In order to maintain the size, colors, and transparent areas of the Photoshop layers, make sure Import Options, Pixel-Aspect is set to 601, Color Levels are set to RGB, Alpha is set to Invert Existing, turn off Import Sequential Files, and set the duration to whatever you want.

● TV Guides

If you prefer to create an image or title from scratch in Adobe Photoshop, guides can help you draw within action-safe and title-safe areas. Photoshop CS includes presets with guides that are already drawn for you. For Avid Xpress Pro, use the Preset called "NTSC D1 720×486 (with guides)." For Avid Xpress DV, use "NTSC DV 720×480 (with guides)."

In Photoshop 7 or earlier, you can create your own document with action-safe and title-safe guides:

❶   Choose File>New.

❷   Specify the starting size. For Xpress Pro, Avid suggests you use 648×486. For Xpress DV, 640×480 pixels.

❸   Set Resolution to 72 ppi, Mode to RGB Color, and Contents to White.

❹   With the new document active, enable View>Rulers.

❺   Press Ctrl+A (Cmd+A) to select the entire frame. Choose Select>Transform Selection. Click on the chain to "Maintain aspect ratio," and set either the horizontal or vertical scale to 90 percent.

❻   With View>Snap To>Guides enabled, drag guides from the ruler to each of the four edges of the selection.

❼   With "Maintain aspect ratio" still enabled, set either the horizontal or vertical scale to 80 percent.

❽   Once again, with View>Snap To>Guides enabled, drag guides from the ruler to each of the four edges of the selection.

❾   With the guides in place, save and name the file something like "blank648x486.psd" or "blank640x480.psd" to use it as a template for future images.

When using the template, choose View>Lock Guides to avoid accidentally moving the guides. Also, when saving your document, be sure to Save As so the template file is not altered.

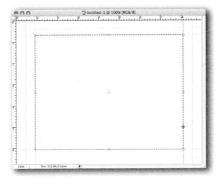

Let It Glow

In the Title tool, to create a glow around your text:

❶ Select your text object with the Selection Tool. (Hint: Alt+ or Option+clicking a text object will toggle between the Selection and Text Tools.)

❷ Set the Shadow Depth Selection value in the lower-right corner to 0.

❸ Click and hold the Shadow Color Selection box to choose a glow color.

❹ Click and hold the Shadow Transparency Selection box to choose the glow's opacity.

❺ Go to the Object menu and choose Preview to see an anti-aliased preview of the text, or press Ctrl+Shift+P (Shift+Cmd+P)

❻ Go to the Object menu and choose Soften Shadow, or press Ctrl+Shift+H (Shift+Cmd+H).

❼ Adjust the Shadow Softness from 4 to 40. If you want to test different values, click Apply instead of OK before committing to a specific value.

Go Away, Mouse

When working in the Title tool, switching back and forth between the Selection tool and the Text tool can involve a lot of mousing. This can be annoying if you hate the mouse. Luckily you can minimize the mouse movement. Instead of mousing away from what you're working on to click on the buttons at the bottom, you can Alt+click (Option+click) on your text object to toggle between the Selection tool and Text tool.

All Together—Kern

You need to check your kerning using the Preview option, which is in the Object menu at the top of the screen. Without Preview turned on, the letters do not quite look like they will when rendered over your final background. If you want to quickly invoke preview, press Ctrl+Shift+P (Cmd+Shift+P).

To have good-looking titles that are easy to read, each letter pair needs to be kerned individually. The goal is to balance the text so it appears even (so if you were to pour water from above, it would flow evenly between each letter pair).

- Text at the top appears as it was typed

- The middle text is much better looking and easier to read than the top example.

- The bottom screenshot is the same as the middle but with Preview enabled.

In order to kern, place your cursor between two letters. Press Alt+Left arrow (Option+Left Arrow) to tighten the spacing. Press Alt+Right arrow (Option+Right Arrow) to loosen spacing.

Toert

Toert

Toert

Bevel's in the Details

We've all seen them—those little, beveled video bugs in the lower-right corner of the screen—usually of some network or cable channel logo. But how can you make one of your own?

1. Create a new full-screen Photoshop document with a transparent background.

2. On the transparent layer, create some text and set its color to 50 percent gray.

3. Apply the Bevel and Emboss layer style and adjust it however you wish.

4. In the Layers palette, set Fill to 30 percent.

5. Save the graphic and import it with Alpha set to Invert Existing.

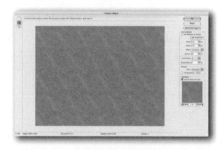

Moving TEXTure Tools

Whether you love or hate its built-in pattern overlays, you can always make your own pattern images to use as moving graphic fills with the help of Avid Pan & Zoom.

❶ First we begin in Photoshop. Open an image you want to turn into a pattern.

❷ Press Ctrl+A (Cmd+A) to select the entire image, and then Ctrl+C (Cmd+C) to copy it to the clipboard.

❸ Create a new, large Photoshop document. Due to limitations of Avid Pan & Zoom, the image cannot exceed 4000×4000 pixels.

❹ Choose Filter>Pattern Maker.

❺ On the right, enable Use Clipboard as Sample and click Generate.

❻ Save this image file.

❼ In Avid, create a title; its color is not important.

❽ Edit the title into a sequence.

❾ Step into the title, and apply Avid Pan & Zoom to the Graphic Fill.

❿ Click the Other Options button in the Pan & Zoom parameters, load the large pattern image, and animate it to your liking. When you step out of the title, the moving pattern will replace the fill color of the text.

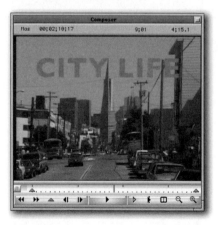

This Text Revised

Here's one way to revise a title without having to enter Effect Mode:

① Park on the title in your sequence and make sure its track is the only one selected.

② Press T to mark that clip and Z to lift it, but leave the In and Out points in place.

③ Control-double-click the title in its bin to revise it in the Title Tool.

④ Save the new title, and it will automatically load in the Source Monitor.

⑤ Press B to overwrite the title to its original spot in the sequence.

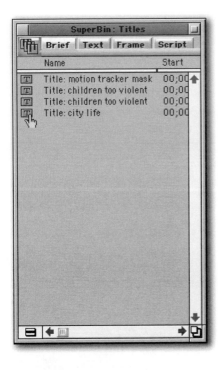

Wish List

What if you have a title with several items in a list and you want to reveal each item one at a time? This technique that is commonly used on the news, in educational programs, and in presentations.

① Begin with a single title with the entire list formatted to your liking.

② Edit the title into the sequence, and enter Effect Mode.

③ Set keyframes for B (or bottom) in the Crop parameters to reveal each list item one by one.

Type-On, Type-Off

A variant of the technique revealing list items, here's how to create a faux type-on effect without requiring third-party products:

❶ Begin with a single title with the word(s) formatted to your liking. This technique works well only with smaller words, so that you will have fewer letters to reveal. Also, and most importantly, the words must be on the same line.

❷ Edit the title into the sequence, and enter Effect Mode.

❸ Set keyframes for R (or right) in the Crop parameters to reveal each letter one by one.

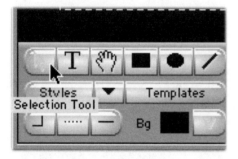

Look Ma No Clicking

How do you switch back and forth between the Selection Tool and the Text Tool? Instead of clicking the Selection Tool and Text Tool buttons at the bottom of the Title Tool, you can Alt+click (Opt+click) on your text object to toggle between the Selection and Text tools.

Gradients

To create a full-screen gradient, use the Square Tool and Rectangle Tool. Draw a rectangle that covers the entire raster, and you can create gradients using Fill Color Blend and Transparency preview.

You Can't Always Get What You Want

Send to Back, Bring Forward, Send Backward, and Send to Front are used to control the layering order of multiple layered text objects. They are also useful if you are having trouble grabbing or selecting a given object because it is obstructed by other objects. Send the obstructing objects behind the one you want to select.

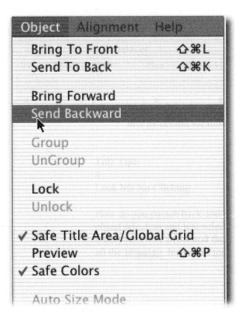

Template Safety

When creating templates, make sure that your text boxes are as long as possible, because when you call up the template to type into it, you cannot alter the size of the text box. You can only type as much text as the text box will hold. This is actually a good thing. Some networks require that text does not violate the far-right corner of the screen, where their network bug sits. So it is good to create a template that has a text box that does not allow text to be typed in this protected area.

Kern with Preview

You can kern individual letter pairs by placing the text cursor in the middle of the pair and using the left- and right-arrow keys while holding down Alt (Option). You need to check your kerning by turning on the Preview option in the Object menu at the top of the screen. Without Preview turned on, the letters do not quite look like they will when rendered over your final background. (Looking at the Title Tool in its regular mode displays aliased type. Preview creates an anti-aliased display that will more closely resemble your finished title.)

Shadowland

When you place type over a moving background, it can be hard to read as the luminosity can change as things move in the scene. Oftentimes, even putting a shadow on a font isn't enough to make it legible when it is keyed over a bright or high-contrast background. To help improve legibility, it is common to put a soft-edged, semitransparent rectangle behind the text. The bad news is that you can't make a soft-edged, semitransparent rectangle using the Rectangle tool. The good news is that you can make a soft-edged, semitransparent rectangular shadow.

❶ Type your text and position it where you want it.

❷ Draw a rectangle (using the Rectangle tool) that covers your text.

❸ Turn the fill transparency of the rectangle to 0.

❹ In the Shadow toolset, pull a small drop-shadow of only a pixel or two. Now you should have your rectangle back in black.

❺ Adjust the transparency of the shadow to about 25 or 30, then go to Object>Soften Shadow (or Ctrl+Shift+H/Cmd+Shift+H) and set the softness to about 20 or 30.

❻ Choose Object>Send to Back or Send Backwards to place the shadow behind the text.

If you need to edit the shadow, you'll need to send the text behind the shadow, so that you can adjust the handles of the rectangle, then send the shadow back behind the text again when you're done.

❶

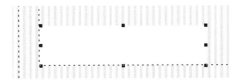

❷

❺

❻

ON THE SPOT

CHAPTER 11

What Was That?

Good audio captivates viewers, bad audio scares them away. Video editors are often strong on the picture side, but lacking in the audio area. It's important to realize that audio is more than 50% of what people "see." It is essential to get your mix right and to smooth out the rough spots—otherwise the viewer has to struggle to comprehend.

Reality television may have lowered the audience's standards for image quality, but the demands for good sound have not diminished. Fix that hum, remove those pops, make the voice dynamic, and get the best mix. Learn to harness the incredible power inside the "box" to engage your audience.

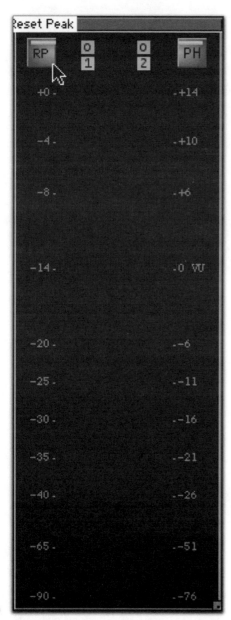

An Audio Console

You may never have considered the console as an audio tool, but it is. If you'd like to see the exact peaks of a specific clip or a section of a sequence, or even an entire sequence, here's what to do:

❶   In the Audio Tool, click on the RP button. This resets the peaks that may have been saved in the Audio Tool LED meters *and* in the console.

❷   Play a clip, sequence, or section of a sequence.

❸   Press Ctrl+6 (Cmd+6) to call up the console.

In the bottom of the console, amidst all of the other minutia is a little table listing the highest peak for each and every track!

Not-So-Free Samples

You can have audio clips with different sample rates in your Xpress Pro sequence, which is very handy indeed. But when it's time to output your sequence you'll need to convert any audio that doesn't match the sample rate of your project.

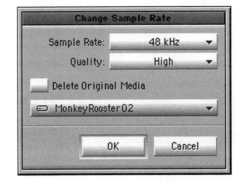

❶   Select your sequence in its bin.

❷   Select Bin>Change Sample Rate. The Change Sample Rate dialog appears.

❸   From the Sample Rate pulldown, select the sample rate of your project (if you're not sure what it is, check your Audio Project settings).

❹   From the Quality pulldown, select High.

❺   If you would like the original clips deleted, check Delete Original Media.

❻   Select the drive you would like the new audio clips written to and click OK.

The non-conforming clips are replaced in your sequence and new audio clips are created in its bin. If you checked Delete Original Media, you'll find that the original audio clips remain in their bins but their associated master clips have been deleted.

Make sure to be aware of any audio in your sequence that is shared with other sequences or projects, such as tracks from a stock music library. If you have any audio of this nature, make sure not to select Delete Original Media.

You'll minimize the time it takes to conform audio sample rates by converting music tracks from CDs at the time of import.

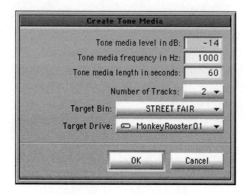

Create Tone Media	
Tone media level in dB:	-14
Tone media frequency in Hz:	1000
Tone media length in seconds:	60
Number of Tracks:	2
Target Bin:	STREET FAIR
Target Drive:	MonkeyRooster01

OK   Cancel

Get Toned

It's always a good idea to put bars and tone at the beginning of your sequence before you output to tape. In fact, it's essential to do so if your tape is bound for television broadcast or will be used as a master to make dupes. Luckily, Xpress Pro can generate tone media for you right from the Audio Tool.

❶   Select Tools>Audio Tool or use the keyboard shortcut Ctrl+1 (Cmd+1).

❷   Click on the Peak Hold (PH) menu button and select Create Tone Media. The Create Tone Media dialog appears.

❸   We recommend keeping the tone media level and frequency at their default settings, but you can change them if you need to.

❹   Set the tone media length. The default of 60 seconds is usually fine.

❺   Set the number of tracks to 2.

❻   Set your target bin and drive and click OK.

Tone media appears as a clip in your target bin. Cut it into your sequence as you would any other audio file.

As for color bars, you'll find a folder called Test_Patterns within the SupportingFiles folder in your Xpress Pro application folder. This folder contains stills of color bars for both NTSC and PAL. Import them to an Xpress Pro bin using the File>Import command.

Stereophonic Bliss (Part 1)

By default, Xpress Pro plays odd-numbered audio tracks through the left channel and even-numbered tracks through the right. You can change Xpress Pro's default left/right channel panning assignment and have it center all of your tracks for you.

❶ In the Project window, click on the Settings tab.

❷ Double-click on Audio. The Audio Settings dialog appears.

❸ Click the circle next to All Tracks Centered so it turns pink, and close the Audio Settings dialog.

Stereophonic Bliss (Part 2)

You can also get creative and use the Audio Mix tool to pan your tracks to taste.

❶ Open the Audio Mix tool by selecting Tools>Audio Mix. This is a good candidate for keyboard mapping, because no keyboard shortcut exists.

❷ Click and hold in the Pan Level field on the audio track you'd like to modify. The Audio Pan Slider appears.

❸ As you continue to hold the mouse button down, adjust the slider to the left or the right to pan the audio track where you want it.

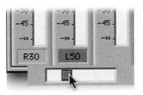

If you want to adjust multiple segments at once, use the Set Pan On Tracks command in the Audio Mix Tool Fast Menu. It applies the pan value of the current segment to its entire track, or a portion thereof. Set In and Out Marks in your Timeline to adjust a portion of the track, or clear any In and Out Marks to adjust it all.

Stereophonic Bliss (Part 3)

The Audio Pan Sliders are convenient but don't offer a particularly fine level of control. For more precise audio panning, use the numeric keypad to enter a value. Click on the Pan Level field and type away as described below. Positive values pan to the right and negative values to the left.

- To pan hard right (all the way to the right channel), type 100, then press Enter (on the numeric keypad, not the Return key).

- To pan hard left, type –100, then Enter.

- To pan to the center, type 0, then Enter.

- You can also center pan by Alt+clicking (Option+clicking) on the Pan Level Field.

You can type in any positive or negative value between 0 and 100, with 50 being halfway between center and hard left/right. Pan tracks to give your audio more dimension. Try placing a sound effect in a specific area of stereo space to emphasize its position on screen.

Lowest Common Denominator

If you've gone the distance and set yourself up with a killer Xpress Pro editing system, you undoubtedly have a nice pair of speakers to monitor your audio. All the subtle nuances (and flaws) of your audio will sound clear as day to you. Most likely, the viewers of your show won't have such nice speakers; they'll be listening to the crappy speakers that most television manufacturers continue to use in their products. For this reason, it's imperative to check your audio on a cheap TV before you output your final cut. That way you can hear exactly what your audience will (or won't) hear and can make any necessary adjustments.

Try laying your show off to VHS and playing it back through the cheapest TV set you can find. We suggest going so far as playing your sequence back through your computer's internal speaker, if it has one. If your audio sounds good this way, you can be confident it'll sound good anywhere!

Adjust the Audio Tool in the Timeline

With limited screen real estate, you may not want to keep the Audio Tool up all the time, but it is definitely a handy item to have. Well, guess what? The little audio LED meters in the Timeline toolbar aren't *just* meters. They give you access to most of the functions of the Audio Tool, including the ability to adjust the output level.

You can adjust the levels on a Mac by Option+clicking the tiny speaker icon. The small button to the right of the meters is the Meter menu, which gives you the rest of the Audio Tool features.

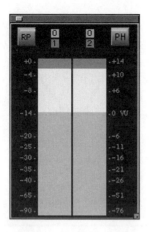

Less Is More

The more audio tracks you have in your sequence, the more difficult it can be to achieve a satisfactory audio mix. It's tempting to keep raising levels here and there, but the more you do this the likelier you are to start residing in audio meter red zone (it's actually more of a light brown in Xpress Pro). When you need to raise the level of something in a mix, try lowering something else instead. Quite often it will have the same effect. It's a trick that professional mixing engineers have used for years. Mixing audio is always a balancing act, so looking at things from all angles can help keep things from swaying too far one way or the other.

Communication Is the Key

It's important to know how the audio on your source tapes was recorded. There are some common techniques, such as recording a lavalier mic on the left channel and a shotgun mic on the right. Sometimes several microphones are recorded on a single channel, and sometimes there are channels with nothing on them at all. The only way you can be sure about what you're hearing is to communicate with your director, cameraman, or audio engineer to find out exactly how they recorded audio to tape. Get them to enter this information on the tape labels, and it'll stay attached to the footage to help everyone down the line in the post-production chain.

Four In One

In many cases you'll need to have more than one of Xpress Pro's principal audio tools open at the same time. This can easily lead to a very cluttered screen, especially if you are editing on a one-monitor system. Well, you need never again suffer this agony as you can toggle between the various audio tools in a single window. With any of the principal audio tools open (Audio Mix, Automation Gain, Audio EQ, or AudioSuite), click on the pulldown menu in the upper-left corner of its window and select which tool you want see. Toggle back and forth from here, instead of opening each tool individually.

Bring It Up /Pro Special\

Eventually you'll have to deal with an audio clip that just wasn't recorded loud enough. Even when you raise the track's level to the maximum in the Audio Mix or Automation Gain Tool, it still won't cut through the clutter. An easy way to increase the volume of a track that isn't loud enough is to double it. Copy and paste the same audio clip into another audio track in your Timeline at the same point in time, and its volume will be effectively doubled.

❶ Click the Segment Mode button in the Timeline or press the Segment Mode key on your keyboard.

❷ Click on the audio segment you wish to double.

❸ Select Edit>Copy or use the keyboard shortcut Ctrl+C (Cmd+C).

❹ Make sure there is an audio track with empty space below your highlighted segment. You may need to add another audio track by selecting Clip>New Audio Track.

❺ While holding down Option (Control), drag your highlighted segment to the empty space on the track below.

❻ Move the Position Indicator to the first frame of your highlighted segment and select Edit>Paste, or Ctrl+V (Cmd+V). The segment is pasted back in its original track.

You now have two copies of the same audio segment at the same point in time in your Timeline. Make sure you leave Segment Mode when you're done by clicking the Segment Mode button.

They Went Thataway ⟨Pro Special⟩

Xpress Pro lets you keyframe audio levels to change the levels of your audio tracks over time. Unfortunately, it does not let you keyframe your audio channels' pan assignments. As an example, let's say you wish to have the audio of an actor who is walking across the screen left to right follow her as she moves. An effective technique for this is to fake a keyframed pan by using dissolves.

1 Make sure the audio tracks you want to affect are the only ones selected.

2 Using the Add Edit button in the Timeline toolbar or the Add Edit key on your keyboard, add an edit to your audio where you want the animated pan to begin and another where you want it to end.

3 Use Add Edit to divide this newly created segment into five segments of equal length.

4 Open the Audio Mix Tool by selecting Tools>Audio Mix.

5 In the Audio Mix Tool, assign pan values for the five new segments as follows:
- Segment 1–L100
- Segment 2–L50
- Segment 3–MID
- Segment 4–R50
- Segment 5–R100

You will need to advance the position indicator to the next segment in order to change its pan value.

6 Using the Quick Transition button in the Timeline or the Quick Transition key on your keyboard, add a 30-frame dissolve, centered on cut, between each of the five segments.

7 Play back your keyframed pan to see how it sounds.

Depending on the duration of the audio, you might need to create more than five segments, or make the dissolve duration shorter or longer, but with a little tweaking you'll have audio that follows your actor across the screen. This is just one example, but once you get the hang of it you'll be able to keyframe audio pans for all types of situations.

Mmm, Mmm, Bad △Pro Special

All too often, we get source tapes with a hum on the audio tracks. Noise from the AC circuit can easily infiltrate an audio cable during recording and cause this annoyance. If this happens to you, here's an easy way to get rid of it:

1 In your Timeline, select the audio tracks with the offending hum.

2 Park the position indicator somewhere within the segments from which you'd like to remove the hum.

3 Open the Audio EQ Tool by selecting Tools>Audio EQ.

4 Click on the Audio EQ Tool Fast Menu, and select NTSC Hum Buster or PAL Hum Buster, depending on which standard your footage was recorded.

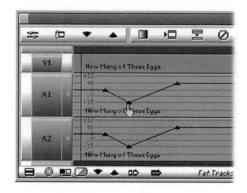

Rubber Bands, Man!

Rubber band keyframes make it easy to control your audio levels without ever leaving the Timeline. It's better than adding segment edits and dissolves to raise or lower the audio on a track—you get much more control with keyframes. If you want to move those keyframes around in time, though, you'll need to use a modifier key:

- To move Rubber Band keyframes left and right, hold down Alt (Option) while you click and drag the keyframe left and right.

- To snap your Rubber Band keyframes to the audio reference lines in the Timeline track, hold down Ctrl (Cmd) as you click and drag the keyframe up and down.

Modify Me

In many cases, holding down a modifier key such as Alt, Option, Cmd, or Control while clicking on a button, slider, or field performs hidden functions. We encourage you to poke around for yourself as you'll discover all sorts of ways to save yourself mouse clicks and menu picks. Here are a few in the Audio Mix Tool that we find useful:

- Alt+click (Option+click) on a level slider or volume level field to reset it to 0.

- Alt+click (Option+click) on a pan level field to pan it center (Mid).

- Alt+click (Option+click) on a slider's track number to select which track is assigned to that slider.

Menu du Jour

The Audio EQ Tool has a Fast Menu that contains some very useful preset templates. You can add your own templates to that menu to build a library of preset EQs that can really save the day when you've got limited time to sweeten your audio. Consider building a library of templates for different types of microphones, voices, and background noises.

When you achieve an EQ setting that you want to save, do the following:

1 Park the position indicator over the segment in your Timeline that has your desired EQ applied to it.

2 Make sure the track that your EQ is applied to is turned on. You should turn off other audio tracks if they also contain EQs at that point in your Timeline.

3 Open the Audio EQ Tool by selecting Tools>Audio EQ.

4 Select File>Open Bin, or use the keyboard shortcut Ctrl+O (Cmd+O). Depending on your platform, do one of the following:

- If you are on a PC, navigate to Program Files/Avid/Avid Xpress/Supporting Files/Site_Effects".

- If you are on a Mac, navigate to Applications/Avid Xpress Pro/Supporting Files/Site_Effects.

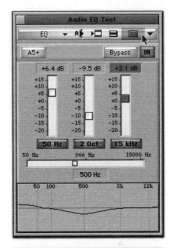

5 Open the file Site_EQs_Bin.avb. The Site EQs bin opens.

6 Drag the purple effect icon from the EQ tool to the Site EQs bin, and close the bin when finished.

Your new EQ template is now listed in the Fast Menu, and you can access it from any project.

Suite Menu

You can use the same steps to save AudioSuite effect templates to the AudioSuite Tool Fast Menu. Just open Site_AudioSuite_Bin.avb from the Site_Effects folder, instead of Site_EQs_Bin.avb.

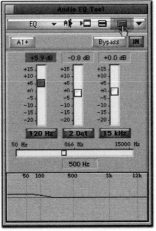

Mix It Live /Pro Special\

Perform dynamic adjustments to your audio tracks by using the Audio Loop Play button. It's found in the four main audio tools and lets you loop a section of audio while you "turn the knobs" to find that perfect level, pan, or EQ setting. We find this feature particularly useful when we're trying to isolate a frequency in the Audio EQ Tool.

- Select the section of audio you wish to loop by setting In and Out marks in your Timeline.

- If you set no marks, Xpress Pro will loop the audio segment closest to the position indicator.

- Monitor as few tracks as possible to get the fastest response.

- When you make an adjustment, it might take a few seconds for the change to become audible. This will vary based on the speed of your computer and how many tracks you are monitoring.

- Use the Bypass button to make a before-and-after comparison.

Listening to the same bit of audio over and over again might drive you crazy, but it's often the best way to fine-tune a mix to perfection.

Hidden Agenda

In Xpress Pro, the master output volume control is well hidden in the Output tab of the Audio Project Settings dialog. If you output only to DV via FireWire, then you should really never change its default setting of 0. You'll get optimal quality this way. In fact, it's really easy to cause distortion by making even minor adjustments. That having been said, you can use it to raise or lower your master output level if you're ready to lay off to tape and the whole thing is just too quiet or loud. Just don't say we didn't warn you!

If you're outputting to analog tape via Mojo or a D/A converter, then you might need to make adjustments here. To access the master Output Gain control:

❶ In the Project window, click on the Settings tab.

❷ Double click on Audio Project. The Audio Project Settings dialog appears.

❸ Click the Output tab.

❹ Adjust the master audio output level by using the Output Gain slider or by typing a value into the Output Level field.

If your deck has audio meters, make sure to set its input level, and Xpress Pro's output level, as you play a reference tone from your Xpress Pro sequence.

Don't confuse the Output Gain control with the Master Volume control. Output Gain affects the volume of what's going to tape, while Master Volume affects the volume of what's going to your computer's speakers.

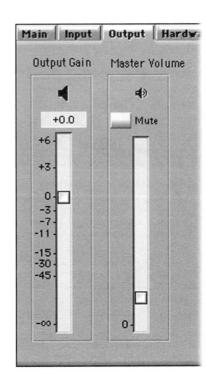

Stark Comparison

Mixing audio for long periods of time fatigues the ears. Eventually your aural perception starts to change. With this fatigue comes the tendency to start cranking up audio levels. When you find yourself in this situation, lay off a section of your show to tape, play it back through your home TV, and compare it to some other content such as a DVD movie, or even a television broadcast. This will give you a sense of the overall volume and EQ of your mix relative to what your audience is used to hearing. Is your mix too loud? Too soft? Is the dialogue buried under the music? It's a good reality check to take, especially when you've been in the Xpress Pro driver's seat a bit too long.

London Calling (Part 1)

Simulate the sound of a voice coming through a telephone receiver without ever using a phone:

❶ In your Timeline, park the position indicator over the segment of audio you wish to make sound like it's coming through a telephone.

❷ Make sure your segment's track(s) are turned on.

❸ Open the Audio EQ Tool by selecting Tools>Audio EQ.

❹ Click on the Audio EQ Tool's Fast Menu and select Telephone EQ 'A'.

❺ Click the Audio Loop button to listen to the results. Depending on the speed of your system, you may need to render the EQ first by clicking the Render Effect button.

You can also try Telephone EQ 'B' and see which works best for your particular audio segment.

London Calling (Part 2)

The Telephone EQ presets mimic the telephone-voice-sound by cutting low and high frequencies while boosting the midrange. You can reverse this to remove the telephone-voice-sound from audio. The Telephone EQ 'B' preset cannot be edited, so here's how do it with Telephone EQ 'A':

❶   Apply the Telephone EQ 'A' preset to your audio using the steps listed in the first half of the tip.

❷   Set the three EQ sliders as follows (from left to right):

   • 1st slider: +15dB

   • 2nd slider: -10.5dB

   • 3rd slider: +15dB

Take a look at the EQ graph. It's now a mirror-image of where you started from.

As with any EQ, the exact settings will vary depending on the characteristics of your source audio. This should get you in the ballpark, then use Audio Loop Play while you tweak the sliders to fine-tune.

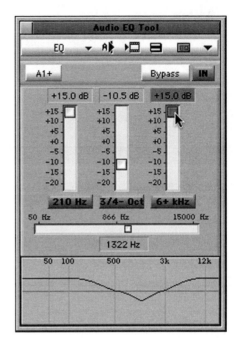

The Baby with the Bathwater

Performing an audio mixdown is necessary if you want to monitor more than eight tracks of audio at once (the most Xpress Pro allows). Mixing down is also a common workaround for the 1-AudioSuite-Effect-Per-Segment limitation. This is all fine and dandy until the time comes that you need to recapture footage or output an EDL. You won't be able to, as tape name and timecode information get thrown out when the mixdown takes place. To save yourself from having to manually search for that missing bit of footage later on, save a pre-mixdown version of your sequence. Since it will still contain all your original audio segments, with their related tape names and timecode locations, you can refer to it should the need arise.

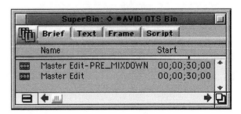

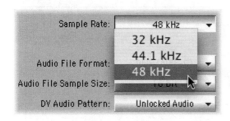

A Sampling of Sample Rates

Working in Xpress Pro, you'll most commonly deal with audio material that's sampled at 48kHz, 44.1kHz, and 32kHz. Here's what you need to know:

- Audio from a camcorder that was set to record at 16-bit has a sample rate of 48kHz.

- Audio from a camcorder that was set to record at 12-bit has a sample rate of 32kHz.

- Audio tracks from a CD have a sample rate of 44.1kHz.

- You should always set your camcorder to record at 16-bit.

- You should always set your Xpress Pro project's sample rate to 48kHz unless your source audio is predominantly 32kHz.

- When importing tracks from audio CDs, always click Yes when asked if you want Xpress Pro to perform the sample rate conversion, unless time is a factor (you'll have to convert them before output anyway, so you may as well get it out of the way now).

Your Free Music Librarian

Now that iTunes is cross-platform, all Xpress Pro users can use it to create a killer production music library. And unlike a real librarian, this one works for free. It automatically loads track info for most stock music library CDs. It can also sample-rate-convert your CD audio tracks from 44.1kHz to 48kHz as it imports them, to save you from having to convert upon import into Xpress Pro (you can set this up in the Importing section of the iTunes Preferences dialog). We use it to create playlists of music selects and burn them to CDs for our clients. We also use it to encode MP3s to email to our graphic artist when she needs to sync an animation to a piece of audio from our Xpress Pro sequence.

Global Warming /Pro Special\

Set a global level for your entire track by using the Set Level On Track command in the Audio Mix Tool Fast Menu. It sure beats adjusting the level on each track segment individually.

1 To make a global adjustment, clear any In and Out marks in your Timeline. To adjust just a portion of the Timeline, select it by setting In and Out marks.

2 Park your position marker over any audio segment within the range you wish to adjust.

3 Open the Audio Mix Tool by selecting Tools>Audio Mix.

4 In the Audio Mix Tool, enable your desired track by clicking on its Track Number button so it turns purple. Repeat for any additional tracks you'd like to adjust.

5 Set the desired level on your tracks.

6 Click on the Audio Mix Tool Fast Menu and select Set Level On Track–Global if you are making a global adjustment or Set Level On Track–In/Out if you've set In and Out marks.

The level adjustment is now applied to your entire track or a portion of it. You can use the same steps to make a global pan setting by using the Set Pan On Track command, also found in the Audio Mix Tool Fast Menu.

Similar commands can be found in the Fast Menus of the Automation Gain, Audio EQ, and AudioSuite tools. Familiarize yourself with them, because they're the best way to apply adjustments or effects to large groups of audio segments.

Play That Funky Music ◿Pro Special◣

If you can tap a beat on the table, you can cut video to music in Xpress Pro. All you need to do is play the music from your Timeline as you tap the beat on the Add Edit key. Cutpoints will be created, synchronized with the music, and you can drop in pieces of video to snap-to the rhythm of your soundtrack.

- Start with a sequence that has your music already edited into it.

- Make sure you have an empty video track above your music. If needed, add a new one by selecting Clip>New Video Track or using the keyboard shortcut Ctrl+Y (Cmd+Y).

- Make sure the Add Edit key is mapped to your keyboard. It's the H key by default.

- Turn off all tracks but the empty video track, otherwise you'll create cut points on them as well.

Click the Play button, and as your music plays tap the rhythm on the Add Edit key (don't click the Add Edit button on the screen–that will stop playback). At the end, what you'll have is a video track of filler segments all timed to the beat of your music. Replace each segment with video of your choosing, and you've got a perfect rhythmically-timed edit!

Silence Is Golden

Audio recorded on analog tape always has a certain degree of tape hiss. In best cases it's virtually inaudible; in worst cases it can sound like your audio was recorded in a snakepit. Use Xpress Pro's Tape Hiss Filter to remove it, and your audio will enjoy a step up in quality:

1. Park the position indicator over a segment where you wish to remove tape hiss.

2. Make sure the tracks for your segment are turned on and other audio tracks are turned off.

3. Open the Audio EQ Tool by selecting Tools>Audio EQ.

4. Click on the Audio EQ Tool's Fast Menu and select Tape Hiss Filter.

Listen to the results. Chances are this will have fixed the problem. Since the Tape Hiss Filter cuts high-end frequencies, you may experience the side-effect of unwanted drop-off in high end. If that's the case, try the Tape Hiss Filter with High End Boost EQ preset instead. It's not always as effective as the basic Tape Hiss Filter but can be a useful alternative.

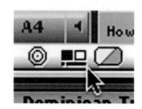

Start at the Source

We always advise on getting as much work done up front as possible. If you've captured or imported audio that you know you'll need to apply level, panning, or EQ adjustments to and you've got some time on your hands before editing begins, apply adjustments directly to the source clips. It's one way of giving yourself a head start.

❶   Load the clip you wish to adjust into the Source Monitor by double-clicking it in its bin.

❷   Click the Toggle Source/Record in Timeline button, which can be found in the lower left of the Timeline window. The source clip's tracks appear in the Timeline.

❸   Apply any desired adjustments in the Audio Mix, Automation Gain, or Audio EQ tools. All of these tools are accessible from the Tools menu.

Remember to click the Toggle Source/Record in Timeline button again when you're finished so your sequences, instead of your sources, will appear in the Timeline window.

You can also apply AudioSuite effects to your source audio clips. Drag the clip from its bin to the AudioSuite window (this works only with master clips, not subclips).

Even Steven

A source audio clip with uneven levels can make your life miserable. This is a common problem with talking head footage. Professional voiceover artists know how to keep the volume of their voice consistent, but for everyone else there's usually some variance in audio level. Instead of having to set tons of audio level keyframes to fix this, use the AudioSuite Compressor. It narrows the dynamic range of your source audio to remove spikes or dropouts in audio level. For a quick fix, there's a preset for uneven levels in a voice recording:

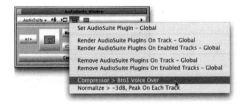

1. Park the position indicator over a segment of audio that contains uneven levels.

2. Make sure the tracks for your desired segments are turned on and other audio tracks are turned off.

3. Open the AudioSuite Tool by selecting Tools>AudioSuite.

4. Click on the AudioSuite Fast Menu and select Compressor>8to1 Voice Over.

5. Render by clicking the Render Effect button at the top of the AudioSuite window.

When Background Noise Is Good

We've included some tips in this section to help you remove unwanted noise from your audio tracks. That being said, background noise is an inherent part of any audio recorded in the field. When you cut together a string of sound bites, for example, your sequence will probably have gaps in the audio tracks. During those gaps, things may sound too quiet as the background noise from the original environment is gone. You can smooth out these gaps by filling them with room tone, which is audio of the room, or environment, where the recording took place.

Experienced audio engineers always record room tone at the end of a session. Sometimes this will be listed on a shot log, and sometimes you can identify it by finding video of a microphone or mic boom, which indicates that room tone is present on the audio. Sometimes you have to locate it by scrubbing to the end of a tape and finding it there. In any case, you should find out if it was recorded, and even if it wasn't you might be able to find a few dead seconds within your source audio and use that.

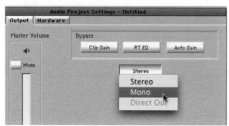

Mono-a-Mono

You should determine at the beginning of your project whether your final audio output will be stereo (two channels) or mono (one channel). Once you make a decision, try to stick with it. If you start one way and then switch horses midstream, your relative audio levels will change and you could very well be faced with the task of adjusting the levels of every audio segment in your sequence.

Set your project to stereo or mono in the Audio Project Settings dialog:

❶　In the Project window, click on the Settings tab.

❷　Double-click Audio Project. The Audio Project Settings dialog appears.

❸　Click on the Output tab.

❹　Choose Stereo or Mono by clicking on the Mix Mode Selection button to toggle.

One case where it makes sense to temporarily switch to mono is if you are laying off a stereo sequence to a mono VHS deck. Remember that levels will shift, but at least you'll be able to get both channels of audio onto your tape.

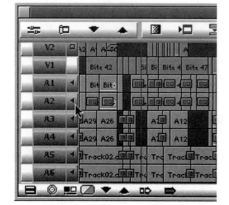

Step Up and Take a Solo

You've got multiple audio tracks but just want to monitor one or two of them. The obvious way to do this would be to turn off the audio tracks you don't want to monitor by clicking on their speaker icons in the Timeline, but this will be a major pain if you have loads of 'em. You'd have to turn them all off individually and then turn them all back on again. A much easier way is to Ctrl+click (Cmd+click) on the speaker icon for the tracks you wish to solo. This turns the speaker icon green for the tracks you've soloed. To monitor all your tracks again, simply click on the one of soloed tracks.

Mixing It Live (Part 1) /Pro Special\

Xpress Pro's Automation Gain Tool lets you mix your audio tracks live as your sequence plays. It records any level adjustments you make by creating keyframes. This feature really comes in handy when you want to ride the levels to produce a perfect audio mix, but it also can create an unfathomable quantity of keyframes. Here's how to do it without creating an overabundance of those little black triangles.

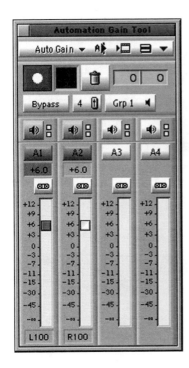

❶ Select the section of audio you want to mix live by setting In and Out marks in your Timeline.

❷ Open the Automation Gain Tool by selecting Tools>Automation Gain.

❸ Select which tracks you want to mix by clicking on their Track Selection buttons so they turn purple.

❹ Select which tracks you want to monitor by clicking on their speaker icons so they turn purple. The fewer tracks you monitor, the better your tool response will be.

❺ Click the Record button in the Automation Gain Tool.

❻ As your sequence plays back, adjust the level slider(s) to mix your audio in real time. When your Out mark is reached, playback stops.

❼ Click on the Automation Gain Tool Fast Menu to list its contents.

❽ Select Filter Automation Gain On Track—In/Out. This reduces the newly created keyframes to a manageable amount.

To give yourself some lead-in time, set a preroll amount (in seconds) in the Automation Gain Tool Preroll field before you start recording. It's directly to the right of the Trash icon.

Mixing It Live (Part 2)

The mouse can be in only one place at a time, and thus you can ride only one audio level fader at a time. If you want to be able to mix more than one track at a time, consider investing in a MIDI-compatible audio mixer or automation controller such as the Avid-qualified JL Cooper FaderMaster Professional or the Digi002 control surface from Digidesign. The hardware faders on these devices control the level sliders in Automation Gain, and you can manipulate up to eight tracks at the same time. If you use audio production software such as ProTools, you can use this device with that as well.

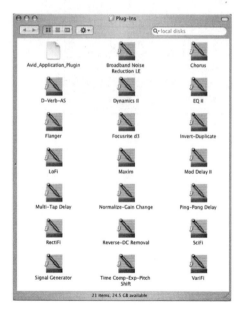

Audio Sweetness

A handful of AudioSuite plug-ins are included with Xpress Pro, but you don't have to stop there. Loads of third-party developers make them, and you can choose from things like sci-fi sound effects, advanced EQs, and voice enhancement filters. Even though AudioSuite plug-ins are generally designed for Pro Tools, you can use many of them with Xpress Pro as well. A good place to start is with the demo plug-ins included on the Xpress Pro installer CD. You'll find it in the Goodies folder. Run the installer, and take 'em for a test drive. A comprehensive list of what's available can be found on the Digidesign web site. They're the division of Avid that makes Pro Tools. Go to www.digidesign.com and follow the link to Developers, then Plug-In Info.

Squeaky Clean

A good companion to Xpress Pro is Bias SoundSoap, an audio cleaning solution that's geared to make your sound squeaky clean. It's one of those tools we turn to in a deadline crunch, since it does most of the work automatically. Tape hiss, buzzing, hum, rumble, and most other types of background noise can be eliminated with a single click of the Learn Noise button. Since SoundSoap is a standalone tool, it can also be used to clean audio for other applications, not just Xpress Pro. Go for a test wash at www.bias-inc.com/products/soundsoap.

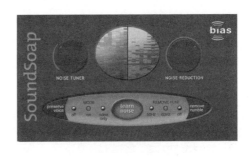

A New Duration

Editing can sometimes feel like assembling a jigsaw puzzle—it's a challenge to get all the pieces to fit together. Sometimes a piece of audio just won't fit, such as a voiceover or music track that needs to fit precisely in a 30-second spot. When this happens, use the Time Compression Expansion plug-in in the AudioSuite window.

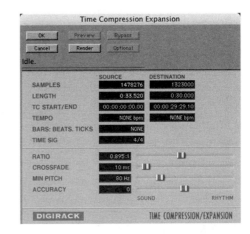

1. Park the position indicator within the segment of audio you'd like to compress or expand.

2. Make sure your desired audio tracks are turned on, and all others are off.

3. Open the AudioSuite tool by selecting Tools>AudioSuite.

4. Click on the Plug-In Selection Menu and select Time Compression Expansion.

5. Click the large purple plug icon to open the Time Compression Expansion controls.

6. In the Destination Length field (the second field from the top in the right column), type in the desired length of your audio segment in the format mm:ss. For example, if you want a duration of 1 minute and 30 seconds, type 01:30.

7. Click OK to close the Time Compression Expansion window.

8. Click the Render Effect button in the AudioSuite Window.

Time Compression Expansion works best with minor adjustments, such as compressing a 62-second segment to fit 60 seconds. If you compress or expand a segment too far, the results are usually not very good.

195

ON THE SPOT

Digitally Outstanding

You've crafted the perfect show, you're happy, the client's happy. You have two choices, have everyone over to your edit room to watch it, or learn to output and share those files. Your Avid has lots of options for sharing with others, and learning to take advantage of them will make your job easier.

We'll tackle going to the Web and making DVDs, and you'll learn how to export still images for print and the Web. We'll cover numerous strategies to share and distribute you work. Plus, we'll show you how to build templates to streamline the process.

Just Whatcha Need

When you want to export a portion of a sequence, it's just a matter of setting In and Out marks in the Timeline and selecting Use Marks in your Export Settings. If Use Marks is not selected, Xpress Pro will export your entire sequence, so make sure you have this set correctly before you export.

You can export selected tracks from your sequence by making sure they're the only ones turned on and selecting Use Enabled Tracks in your Export Settings. Turning Use Enabled Tracks off will export all of the tracks in your sequence.

Squeeze It!

Xpress Pro has the ability to export directly to QuickTime with the Sorensen 3 codec. Sorenson 3 is by far the best QuickTime codec to use for web streaming, but you'll get much better results if you use Sorenson Squeeze, which is included with Xpress Pro. Squeeze can accept a QuickTime Reference movie from Xpress Pro and has advanced features such as 2-Pass VBR encoding and numerous pre-processing filters. You can also use it to batch-encode for multiple bit-rates. If you're on Windows, then Squeeze can also encode MPEG-2 files for DVDs. In a pinch, Squeeze can even encode directly from a tape in your DV deck or camcorder via FireWire.

For Future Reference

When you need to export a QuickTime movie from Xpress Pro for use in a QuickTime-compliant third-party application, save yourself some time and disk space by exporting a QuickTime Reference file. QuickTime Reference files don't contain the actual media. They're just pointers that allow QuickTime to read your Avid OMF media. Since QuickTime Reference files need to access the original OMF media, you can use them only on the same computer or network as your Xpress Pro media drives. Here's how to create an Export Setting for QuickTime Reference files:

❶ In the Project window, click on the Settings tab.

❷ Scroll down to Export (you may have more than one Export setting).

❸ Click on any Export setting to highlight it.

❹ Select Edit>Duplicate, or use the keyboard shortcut Ctrl+D (Cmd+D).

❺ Rename the new setting by clicking in the field to the right of it so a cursor appears. Type "QuickTime Reference" and press Return.

❻ Double-click on your new QuickTime Reference export setting. The Export Settings dialog appears.

❼ From the Export As pulldown menu, select QuickTime Reference.

❽ From the Defaults menu, select Digital Mastering.

❾ If you will be using the reference file on another computer on your network, click in the box next to Use Network Media References so a checkmark appears.

❿ Make sure there's a checkmark in the box next to Use Avid DV Codec. If not, click in the box so a checkmark appears.

⓫ Click OK.

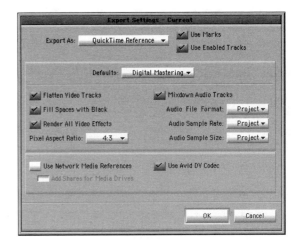

When you are ready to export your QuickTime reference, make sure that your new QuickTime Reference Export Setting is active by clicking to the left of it in the Project window so a checkmark appears.

Moving It Away (Part 1)

QuickTime Reference files are great if you'll be using them on the same computer or network as your Xpress Pro system, but if you'll be moving the file somewhere else you'll need to export a self-contained QuickTime Movie. Self-contained QuickTime Movies can be played back on any system that has QuickTime and the appropriate Avid codec installed. Here's how to create an export setting for self-contained QuickTime movies:

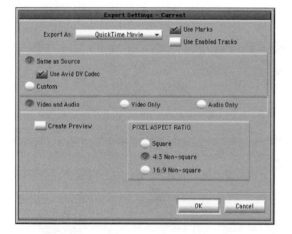

❶ In the Project window, click on the Settings tab.

❷ Scroll down to Export (you may have more than one Export setting).

❸ Click on any Export setting to highlight it.

❹ Select Edit>Duplicate, or use the keyboard shortcut Ctrl+D (Cmd+D).

❺ Rename the new setting by clicking in the field to the right of it so a cursor appears. Type "QuickTime Movie" and press Return.

❻ Double-click on your new QuickTime Movie export setting. The Export Settings dialog appears.

❼ From the Export As pulldown menu, select QuickTime Movie.

❽ Click in the oval to the left of Same As Source so it turns purple.

❾ Click in the box next to Use Avid DV Codec so a checkmark appears.

❿ Under Pixel Aspect Ratio click the oval to the left of 4:3 Non-square so it turns purple.

Before you click OK to close the Export Settings dialog, select Video and Audio, Video Only, or Audio Only. Depending on what you're exporting, you might need to modify this before the export.

Moving It Away (Part 2)

A computer needs to have the Avid DV QuickTime codec installed on it in order to play back QuickTime movies exported with the Avid DV codec. Avid allows you to freely copy the Avid QuickTime codecs to as many computers as you like. The Xpress Pro installer puts the Avid DV, Avid Meridien Compressed, and Avid Meridien Uncompressed QuickTime codecs in the following location:

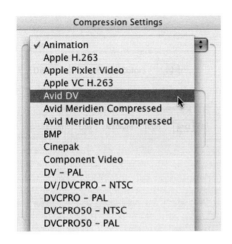

On a PC (Windows/system32):

- "AvidAVdvCodec" is the Avid DV codec.

- "AvidQTAVUI" is the Avid Meridien Uncompressed codec.

- "AvidQTAVJI" is the Avid Meridien Compressed codec.

On a Mac (Library/QuickTime):

- "AvidAVdvCodec.component" is the Avid DV codec.

- "AvidAVUICodec.component" is the Avid Meridien Uncompressed codec.

- "AvidAVDJCodec.component" is the Avid Meridien Compressed codec.

Simply copy the required codecs from your Xpress Pro system to the same directory on the computers that you want to be able to play back your exported QuickTime movies. This will also allow that computer to save and render QuickTime movies to these codecs.

Picture This

You can export stills from Xpress Pro for use in storyboards, on web sites, in DVD menus, or even for the package design of your finished videotape or DVD. We recommend exporting at Xpress Pro's native frame size and resizing the image, if necessary, in an image editing application such as Adobe Photoshop. Here's how to create an Export Setting for still images:

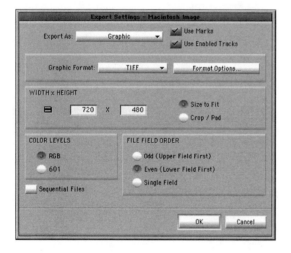

❶ In the Project window, click on the Settings tab.

❷ Scroll down to Export (you may have more than one Export setting).

❸ Click on any Export setting to highlight it.

❹ Select Edit>Duplicate, or use the keyboard shortcut Ctrl+D (Cmd+D).

❺ Rename the new setting by clicking in the field to the right of it so a cursor appears. Type "Still Image" and press Return.

❻ Double-click on your new Still Image export setting. The Export Settings dialog appears.

❼ From the Export As pulldown menu, select Graphic.

❽ From the Graphic Format pulldown, select your still file format of choice. We like to use TIFF because it's lossless and virtually all image editing applications can read it. Make sure to click the Format Options button and set Compression to None.

❾ Set the width and height by typing your corresponding frame size into the text fields

- If you are exporting from NTSC DV, use 720×480

- If you are exporting from NTSC 1:1 or 15:1, use 720×486

- If you are exporting from PAL use 720×576

❿ Click the oval next to Size to Fit so it turns purple, and click OK.

What to State When You Slate

Always put a slate at the beginning of your finished show. It's essential if you're making a master to make dupes from, or if your show is heading to broadcast. It also lets people know who to contact (or yell at) should any issues arise. Things that you should include in your slate are:

- The title of the show
- The length of the show (total running time, or TRT)
- How the audio is mixed (e.g. mono, stereo, discreet tracks, multiple languages)
- Date and/or version
- Director's name
- Editor's name
- Production company
- Contact info

Drop It!

Skip the File>Export command and export by dragging a clip or sequence from its bin to your desktop, to any folder in Windows Explorer on a PC, or the Finder on a Mac. When you do this, the currently active Export Settings apply. Make sure the setting you want is active by clicking to the left of its name in the Project window so a checkmark appears. This is one of the reasons why we recommend creating different Export Settings for different types of file exports. Dragging and dropping is much faster than having to repeatedly select File>Export.

The Tangled Web (Part 1)

When it comes time to get your show on the web, there are several directions you can go in. There are three major streaming media formats (Real, Windows Media, and QuickTime), and your viewers might be watching on anything from a dial-up connection to a corporate LAN. Knowing the characteristics of your viewer's computer and Internet connection speed is ideal, but this sort of information is not always available. To make your show viewable by the widest possible audience, encode it to at least two of the popular streaming formats, and to two bitrates—one for dial-up users and one for users with broadband connections. This way you'll avoid shutting out a viewer if they don't have the appropriate player installed or don't have a fast enough connection to the Internet.

You have several options when it comes to encoding for the web:

- Sorenson Squeeze, included with Xpress Pro, can encode QuickTime movies with the Sorenson 3 codec (the best codec by far for QuickTime on the web).

- The Windows Media 9 Encoder can be downloaded for free at www.microsoft.com/downloads. It runs on Windows only.

- Helix Producer Basic encodes Real files and is also free. Download it at www.realnetworks.com/products/producer/index.html.

- Cleaner, available from Discreet (www.discreet.com), can encode Real, Windows Media, and QuickTime, as well as several other formats. QuickTime Pro can also encode.

If you find yourself having to encode large amounts of video for the web on a regular basis, you might want to consider an industrial-strength multi-format encoder such as Agility from Anystream (www.anystream.com/agility.asp) or Telestream's Flip Factory (www.telestream.net/products/flipfactory.htm).

The Tangled Web (Part 2)

When you decide on your tools of choice for web encoding, here are some recommended encoder settings:

For broadband (cable/DSL) delivery

- Video data rate: 252Kbps

- Frame rate: 15fps

- Frame size: 320×240

- Audio data rate: 48Kbps

- Audio sample rate: 44.1kHz stereo

For dialup delivery

- Video data rate: 24Kbps

- Frame rate: 7.5fps

- Frame size: 160×120

- Audio data rate: 16Kbps

- Audio sample rate: 22.050kHz mono

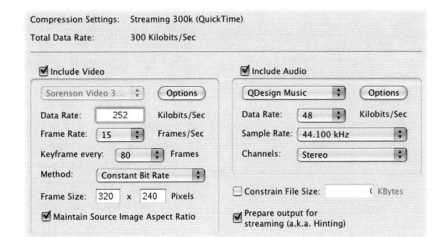

Encoding is always a balancing act between data rate and quality. Higher data rates give better quality, but the higher you go the more risk there is of shutting out viewers with slower connection speeds. You should keep the total data rate (video + audio) to 300kbps or less for broadband and 40kbps or less for dialup. If you're encoding for a corporate LAN you can go much higher (600–800kbps) but we recommend checking with a network administrator to make sure.

The Tangled Web (Part 3)

Traditional video is watched on a television, but streaming video is watched on a computer screen. TVs and computer screens display video in very different ways:

- TVs display interlaced frames, while computers display progressive frames.

- TVs play video at a frame rate of 29.97fps (NTSC) or 25fps (PAL), while computers can theoretically play back video at any frame rate.

- TVs overscan the picture, cropping out about 10 percent of the outer edge of the frame, while computers show the entire frame.

- TVs display colors in the YUV gamut, while computers use RGB.

Since video for the web is watched on a computer screen, as opposed to a TV, pre-processing the video before it is encoded optimizes it for viewing on a computer. If your encoding tool has pre-processing capabilities (also called prefiltering), then make the following adjustments:

- De-interlace the video.

- Crop the video to remove any black areas (blanking) at the edges of the frame.

- Color-expand the video from YUV colorspace to RGB colorspace.

The Disc Preservation Society

Outputting to DVD and CD is pretty standard these days for client delivery, and is a great way to archive your Xpress Pro projects. Like videotape, however, DVD and CD disks don't last forever. Here are a few tips to help give your disks maximum longevity:

- Don't use peel-and-stick labels. The glue will eventually damage the disk, and the label itself can easily jam a CD or DVD player.

- Label your disks with a permanent marker, but don't overdo it. The ink can damage a disk over time, so keep it to a minimum. Several inkjet printers also can print right on discs.

- Store your disks in jewel cases in a cool, dark place.

- Keep disks out of direct sunlight, which will destroy them very quickly.

- Make backup copies of all disks that contain important data.

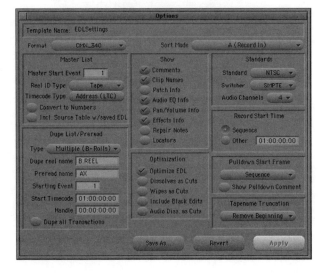

Decisions, Decisions . . .

Xpress Pro is a fine tool for offline editing because its project files are compatible with high-end Avid systems. You can move an Xpress Pro project to a Media Composer or Symphony for online finishing. Another common practice is to online with a traditional tape-to-tape system. If you're going to do this, then you'll need to export an EDL (Edit Decision List) from Xpress Pro. This is a text document containing all the details of your sequence. When you import your EDL into the online system, it'll allow the online editor to easily recreate your offline edit. First, you need to install the Avid EDL Manager from the Other Installers folder on your Xpress Pro installer CD. Once EDL manager is installed:

❶ Highlight the sequence you want to create an EDL for by clicking on it in its bin.

❷ Select Tools>EDL. The EDL Manager opens.

❸ Open the EDL Manager Options Dialog by selecting Window>Options.

❹ Set the output options based on the online system you will be using. If you're not sure, now would be a good time to drop a phone call or e-mail to the online editor. When finished, click the Apply button and close the window.

❺ To create your EDL, click on the arrow pointing to the Update icon. The EDL displays in the text field.

❻ Save your EDL by selecting File>Save As.

Make sure you communicate with the online editor and get the appropriate EDL specs for the system on which they will be creating your online edit. Otherwise you could find yourself with a bunch of useless text and a very unhappy client!

Down and Dirty

Sometimes you've just gotta get a rough cut out to a client right away. In this case, take the low-tech approach and lay your sequence off to VHS. It may not always be pretty, but it's real-time, and it always works. You'll need a FireWire deck/camcorder with passthrough capability (most of them have it), or a DV-to-analog converter, or a Mojo. Here's how to do it without a Mojo:

❶   Attach your FireWire deck/camcorder, or a DV-to-analog converter, to the FireWire port on your Xpress Pro system.

❷   Connect the analog outputs of your FireWire deck/camcorder or DV-to-analog converter to the inputs of your VHS deck.

❸   Click the Toggle Digital Video Out button in the Timeline so it turns from green to blue. This button is in the upper-right corner of the Timeline window next to the Avid logo.

❹   Press record on your VHS deck and play your Xpress Pro sequence.

Remember that real-time effects are disabled when you output with this method.

If you've got a Mojo, connect Mojo's analog outputs to the inputs of your VHS deck and play your sequence as your deck records. With Mojo your real-time effects will still play as you output your sequence. If you find yourself having to output to VHS on a regular basis, it's definitely worth investing in a Mojo for this reason alone.

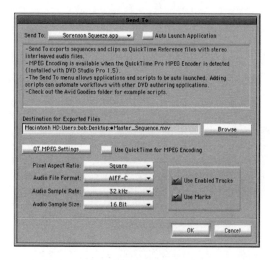

Return to Sender

When you need to export your sequence (or a portion thereof) to a third-party application on your Xpress Pro system, take advantage of the Send To command. Send To performs a QuickTime Reference export, launches the third-party application, and in some cases can load the exported material into that application. Here's how to use it:

1 In your Timeline, set In and Out marks for the portion of your sequence you wish to export. If you want to export the entire sequence, clear any In and Out marks.

2 Select the tracks you wish to export by turning them on, and turning all other tracks off.

3 Highlight the sequence in its bin by clicking on it.

4 Select File>Send To. The Send To dialog appears.

5 Click on the Send To: pulldown menu and select Add Item.

6 Navigate to your third-party application and click OK.

7 Click the box next to Auto Launch Application so a checkmark appears.

You can create scripts to load the exported QuickTime Reference into the third-party app. Sample scripts are included on the Xpress Pro installer CD in the Goodies folder. Load them into the Send To dialog by using the Add Item command as described above.

The Branding Iron

Television networks usually place a bug on the screen to protect their content (it'd be hard to tape a movie off of HBO and not notice the HBO logo sitting there in the corner). You can protect your own content just like the big guys by creating a watermark in Xpress Pro's Title Tool. It's a good idea to watermark review and approve copies of an edit to identify them as such, and we never send out a demo reel without a watermark (so prospective clients know who to call!).

❶ In your sequence, create a new video track by selecting Clip>New Video Track or pressing Ctrl+Y (Cmd+Y).

❷ Open the Title Tool by selecting Tools>Title Tool.

❸ Create a title with your desired text.

❹ Set your title's transparency to 85 percent by clicking-and-holding on the Fill Transparency Selection box and moving the transparency slider to 85.

❺ Select File>Save Title or press Ctrl+S (Cmd+S). Give your title a name, select a target Bin, Drive, and Resolution, and click Save.

❻ Edit the watermark title onto your new video track.

Bits and Gops

Sooner or later you'll have to deliver a show on DVD. MPEG-2 is the file format you'll need to encode your edit to in order to put it on a DVD. Knowing how to adjust your MPEG-2 encoder to get best results is key. Here's the low-down:

- The data rate (bitrate) of MPEG-2 is measured in Mbps (megabits per second). The higher the bitrate, the better the quality.

- Variable bitrate (VBR) encoding usually gives better quality than constant bitrate (CBR) so use it whenever possible. One exception to this is if you plan to create a multi-angle DVD. In this case encode your video at CBR.

- The total bitrate (video + audio) cannot exceed 9.8Mbps. More than 6Mbps chokes most computers.

- MPEG-2 frames are stored as GOPs (Groups of Pictures).

- A DVD chapter marker can only be set at the first frame of a GOP (GOP Header). Many DVD encoding and authoring tools let you force a GOP header on a specific frame. Check the manual for your specific software.

If you're running Windows XP, use Sorenson Squeeze (included with Xpress Pro) to encode your MPEG-2 files. It's got the Main Concept MPEG-2 encoder built-in, which produces excellent quality output. If you're on a Mac, you'll need to get your own MPEG-2 encoder. We like Apple's Compressor, which comes bundled with DVD Studio Pro.

To delve deeper into the world of DVD, check out the DVD FAQ by Jim Taylor, the guru of all things DVD at www.dvddemystified.com/dvdfax.html.

Burn, Baby, Burn!

It's useful to put burned in timecode (timecode that's visible on the screen) on review and approval copies of your show. That way your client can match up his or her notes with timecode locations.

❶ In your sequence, create a new video track by selecting Clip>New Video Track or press Ctrl+Y (Cmd+Y).

❷ In the Project window, click on the Effect Palette tab to reveal the Effect Palette.

❸ In the left-hand column, click on Illusion FX.

❹ In the right-hand column, scroll down until you see the Timecode effect.

❺ Drag the Timecode effect to your new video track.

You can make adjustments to the timecode effect in the Effects Editor.

If you have a Mojo, then the timecode effect will play in real time without rendering. If you've got no Mojo, then you'll have to render. This effect can take quite a while to render, especially if you have a very long show. In this case, consider rendering it overnight or on your lunch break.

ON THE SPOT

Media Management

Media management really describes two things: finding your shots and managing the space you have for media on your drives. We're going to cover both of these important topics in this chapter. We will look at managing media at the Project level, the Bin level, using the Media Tool, and with two important tools: Decompose and Consolidate.

Media management has long been one of Avid's strong suits. The media management capabilities built into your Xpress Pro or Xpress DV are the gold standard for all of the other NLEs on the market, but if you don't know how to take advantage of that power, you're missing out on one of the key reasons to own Xpress Pro.

Of all the chapters in this book, this is probably the one with the least sex appeal ... unless you're turned on by raw power!

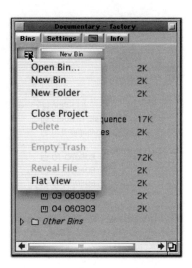

Everything in Its Place

You can organize your Project window by creating folders for grouping bins. For example, if you have several sequence bins—one for old sequences, one for the final sequence, one for selects sequences—then you could create a Sequences folder in which to store all of those various sequence bins. Or maybe, for a documentary, you would have a bin for each interview subject, then have an Interviews folder that would contain all of your interview bins.

- To create a folder in your project, you must be in the Bin tab of the Project window, then choose New Folder from the Project Fast menu.

- To organize bins into folders, simply drag the bins into the folders.

However, if you want to see all of your bins without stepping into the individual folders, choose Flat View from the Project Fast Menu.

It's Easy to Say Goodbye

We've never met a project that we didn't meet again. That's one of the reasons for good media management. But there comes a time to get the old projects out of the system so that your project list isn't too long and so that you aren't depressed about how many projects you've done lately. This is done at the desktop level.

- Locate your Avid Projects folder and archive the project by saving it on some removable media, like a CD or a DVD. Please, oh please, label the darn thing.

- Once it's archived—give an extra copy to your client even—delete the entire project folder.

Clean the Attic

While you're at it, the Attic should be nearby, do a search and destroy on the project in the Attic as well to save on disk space. The Attic is a back-up location for all of your projects. Both the Projects Folders and Attic are in various places depending on your platform and even what version of software you're running. Using a Seach or Find is an easy way to find it without having to remember a file path.

Create an Import Folder in Your Project Folder

At the desktop level, your project is just a simple folder that contains bins and settings. But since it is a regular folder in your computer, you can also add folders to it at the desktop level and put anything you want in that folder. When you want to import things into your project, it is a good idea to first place them in a special import folder inside your project folder. This will make it much easier to archive the project when you are done and will facilitate any batch importing that you may need to do later.

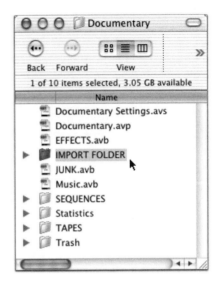

Bin There, Done That

There are many reasons why you may want to use a bin that was created in another project. One of our favorite uses for this is to borrow from a project and a bin called Elements which contains all of the stuff that you use in all of your projects, like bars, tone, countdowns and slates. Open the "Elements" bin into every project you create so that you don't have to recreate all of these elements for every project. Another good use for this is when you have a regular client. You may want to borrow elements from other projects with that same client for use in the current project. Opening a bin from another project is simple.

❶ With the Bin tab active in the Project window, or with any bin active, press Ctrl+O (Cmd+O) or go to the File>Open Bin.

❷ In the Open Bin window, navigate to the bin you want to open, which will be in the project folder from the project in which it was created. Xpress Pro keeps Avid projects in various places, so you could do a Search or Find on the name of the project or bin.

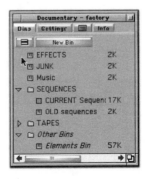

❸ The bin will open inside the application. When you close the bin, it is saved in a folder called Other Bins at the bottom of the list of bins in the Project window.

Sort 'Em First, Shoot Them Later

This may be backwards from what the Navy SEALs in the movies tell you, but when you're editing, your most pressing need in the bin is probably sorting. Force some order on those unruly bins! There are a number of keyboard shortcuts you should learn and use.

- Clicking on a column (heading) in a bin and pressing Ctrl+E (Cmd+E) sorts the bin based on the information in the column. If it is the Name column, it will sort it alphanumerically.

- Clicking on a column (heading) in a bin and hitting Ctrl+Alt+E (Option+Cmd+E) reverse sorts the bin based on the information in the column. If it is the timecode column, it will sort it highest to lowest.

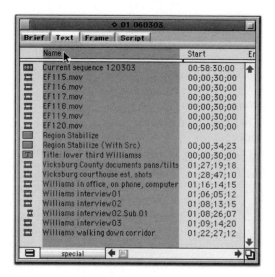
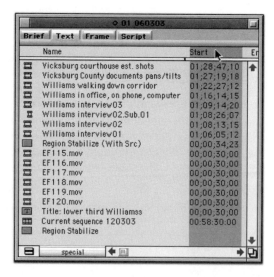

Short Sorts

Sorting functions do not only work alphanumerically. You can also sort the icon column to the far left. When you do this, sequences move to the top like fine cream, then clips, then subclips then titles and then effects. This is an easy way in a big bin to find a sequence. You can also sort on clip color.

You can also do multilevel sorts by Shift-selecting columns (headings) and sorting them using left to right dominance. So if you want to sort group tapes together, then timecodes within those tapes, the tape column has to be to the left of the timecode column. (You can just drag headings for columns into the order you want.)

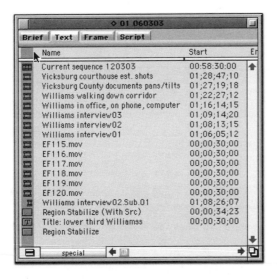
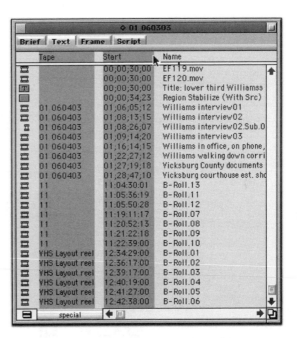

Turn Oscar into Felix. Tidy Your Bins!

Once you've dragged bin headings around and basically made a mess out of your bin, there is no need for a cleaning service or a maid. One simple command can instantly move all of your columns as close as they can get to one another. All you have to do is remember the fairly easy keyboard shortcut: Ctrl+T (Cmd+T).

This is helpful to save screen real estate by cramming the most information into the smallest space. It's also handy when trying to print your bins. If you notice that some columns don't move as close together as you think they should, this is usually because there is a single long name or entry that you can't see currently in the bin. Scroll up and down the bin and you will see that all of the columns are as close as the longest entry allows.

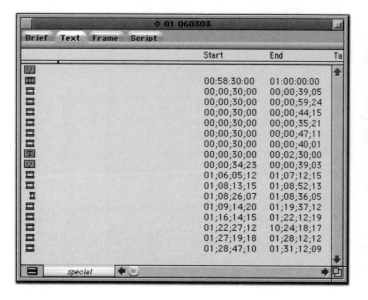

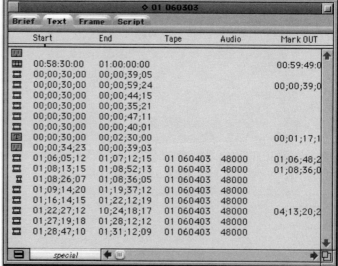

Will It Fit?

If you've got a bin of logged clips and you're wondering whether you've got the space to capture them, the answer is in the Console. The Console will calculate the total time of clips in a bin down to the second.

❶ Select your bin. Make sure that there are no sequences (or the total length of the sequence will be counted) or titles or imported files (because it counts these for their full imported length, which is not really accurate for storage requirements.)

❷ Ctrl+A (Cmd+A) to select all the clips, or lasso the clips you want or Shift-select specific clips.

❸ Once you have all of the clips that you want selected, press Ctrl+I (Cmd+I). This calls up the Console. (The Console can also be called up by itself by pressing Ctrl+6 (Cmd+6).) Inside the Console, the total length is displayed.

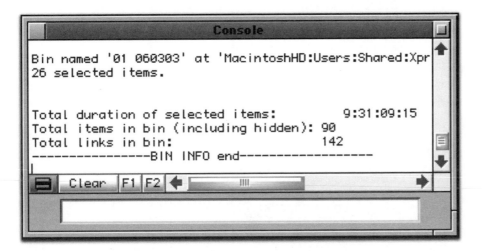

```
Console

Bin named '01 060303' at 'MacintoshHD:Users:Shared:Xpr
26 selected items.


Total duration of selected items:        9:31:09:15
Total items in bin (including hidden): 90
Total links in bin:               142
-------------------BIN INFO end-------------------
```

Clear F1 F2

Check That Sequence

Before you lay off an important master there are several things you do not want in your sequence: offline media, offline resolution video, and improper audio sample rates. But how can you be sure that none of these exist? Very, very easily and very, very quickly.

❶ Drop your sequence into a new bin with nothing else. Or if you already have the current sequence in its own bin with just some miscellaneous flotsam and jetsam, then drag the junk out of the bin, leaving the sequence in the bin by itself.

❷ Click on the bin Fast Menu in the bottom-left corner and pick Bin View from the selections. This calls up the Bin View window.

❸ Near the bottom of the Set Bin Display window, check the box labeled Show Reference Clips and click OK.

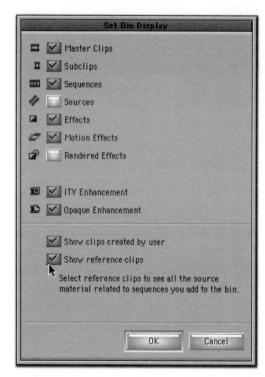

❹ Instantaneously, every clip associated with that sequence fills the bin.

❺ In order to see what clips may be trouble, you need to make sure you are in the Text tab of your bin, so that you can display the headings you need to see. With your bin selected, go to the bin fast menu again and choose Headings.

❻ In the Bin Column Selection window click the All/None button so that all headings are deselected, then click on the Audio, Offline and Video choices. Click OK. You may want to save this bin view as Final Check.

❼ Sort on these columns and scroll through, looking for clips that are offline, wrong resolution, or wrong sample rate.

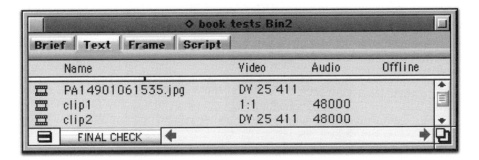

Color Me Impressed

A great media management technique is the ability to color code clips so that spotting them in your bin or sequence is easy. In bins, clip color can either change the color of the clip icon in the bin, or you can call up the Color heading in your bin to see a color chip in the color column. The other advantage to having a Color column is that you can then sort on clip color. You can use clip color to identify footage coming from various stock sources or maybe color code each interviewee. You could also color code based on the section in the sequence in which the clip belongs. There are two ways to add clip color to a clip in the bin.

❶ In your bin, go to the Fast Menu and pick Headings. Add the Color heading and click OK.

❷ Your bin now has a Color column. If you click in the column next to a clip, a pulldown menu appears, giving you color choices for the clip. Pick a color from the list and the clip is automatically coded with that color.

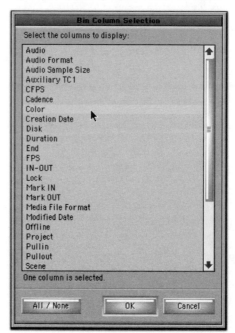

Clip That Again?

You can also color code groups of clips in a bin.

❶   Lasso or Shift-select the clips that will have the same color.

❷   From the Edit Menu, drag to Select Clip Color and hold until a sub-pulldown
menu appears with the clip color list. Select a color, and it will be applied to all of
the selected clips.

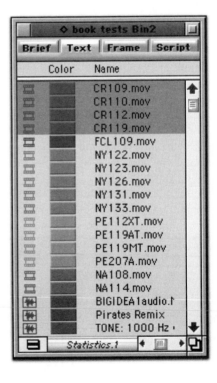

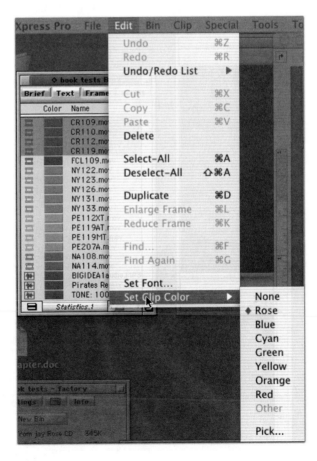

Creating Custom Bin Headings

All of the headings you can choose for your bin views are helpful, but every editor and every project is different, so there's always a need for a column that's not on the list. These are usually the most important headings when it comes to finding the clips that you need. A common custom heading to create is one that rates your clips or to sort based on the kind of shot—WS, MS, CU, XCU. To determine what custom headings to create, think of how you will need to find shots and organize your clips. If you know a show is divided into segments based on the topic of an interview clip, then that is a great custom column: topic.

- To make a custom column, drag the horizontal size of your bin out so that you can see some blank space to the right of the last column. You can also leave your bin size the same and use the horizontal scroll bar to slide down to the last column.

- Drag your cursor along the column names from left to right, and the cursor is an arrow. As you mouse over past the last column, the cursor will change to a text I-beam. Now you can type any column name you wish. To create another custom column, just move a little more to the right and type again.

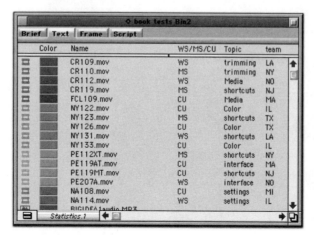
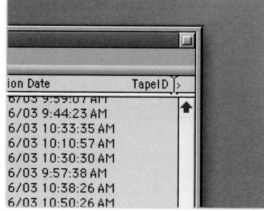

Custom Column Data Entry

Once you've got your custom columns, you'll want to add data into these columns for each clip so they can be sorted and sifted based on that data.

- Making entries in custom columns for clips is simple. Just click in the column area next to the clip and type the info. You want to use the same spellings and spacing and watch for typos because what you're making is actually a database, and sorting and sifting will be alphabetical and numerical.

- Once you have made some entries, Alt+clicking (Option+clicking) in the column calls up a pulldown of all previous entries! This is an excellent way to make sure that you maintain consistency in the way clips in these custom columns are labeled.

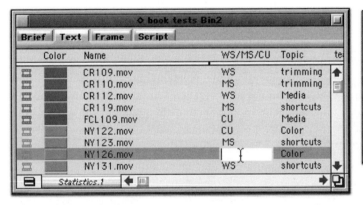
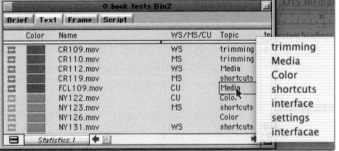

Make It to the Top

Sometimes, you may want a particular clip to sit at the top of your bin, where it is easy to find. (Maybe it's a shot you use over and over or a voice over clip.) But there is no criterion that will allow you to sort it to the top. There is a secret way to do this however.

❶ Switch your bin to Script View.

❷ Drag the clip that you want to relocate all the way up to the top of the list and drop it there.

❸ Switch back to Text or Brief View and there it sits, right where you want it.

If you re-sort the bin after dragging the clip to this position, the clip will be re-sorted back into whatever position the sort is supposed to execute.

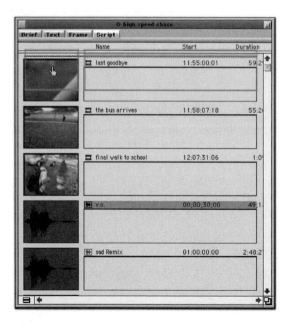

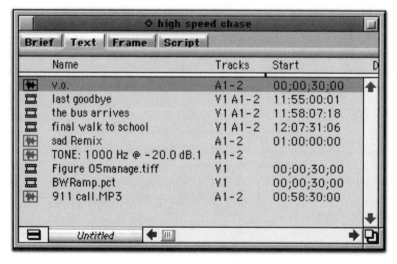

Lock 'Em Up

If you fear that someone will accidentally delete some of your footage—even if the most likely culprit is you—there is a way to lock clips so that they cannot be deleted from within the application. Obviously if you run a degausser over your hard drive, the locks won't do anything to save them, but you protect yourself from most levels of carelessness. Using locks is especially smart on footage that you use over and over or footage that you know you want for another project and you want to make sure that when the current project media gets deleted, this stuff gets saved.

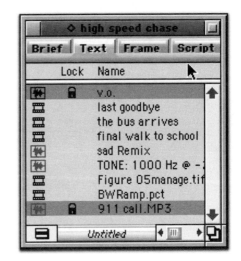

❶   In your bin, select the clip or clips that you want to lock. You can use any of the common methods such as Shift-selecting or lassoing for multiple clips.

❷   From the Clips menu, choose Lock Bin Selection.

❸   If you want to see which clips are locked, in the Bin menu, choose Headings and in the Bin Column Selection window that appears, choose Lock, and click OK.

❹   Now your bin will have a column that displays a small padlock icon next to any locked items.

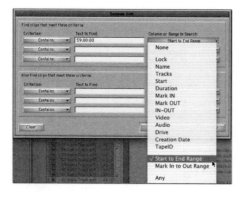

Find That Timecode

If you edit with a producer in the room, you are probably often asked to find a clip with a specific timecode. With very large projects this is sometimes difficult. There are two things that can make this search a quick one.

Item One

❶ Create a master bin that holds all of the clips. The easiest way to do this is to choose Media Tool from the Tools Menu.

❷ Choose All Drives and Current Project and Master Clips from the available buttons. This calls up every master clip in your project.

❸ Create a new bin and drag all of the clips in the Media Tool to the new bin. Name it "Master Bin."

Item Two

❶ With your Master Bin populated with all of your clips, go to the Bin Menu and choose Custom Sift. This menu selection is also available from the bin Fast Menu.

❷ Type the desired timecode into the first text entry box and choose Start to End Range from the Column or Range To Search pulldown menu.

❸ Click Apply or OK, and your bin will only display the clip or clips that contain that specific timecode somewhere within the clip. Total elapsed time: about 10 seconds (assuming that you had already made your master bin while you were waiting for the producer to get off the phone).

❹ To unsift, go to the Bin Menu and choose Show Unsifted.

Decompose

To "upres" a sequence from an offline resolution, it is possible to select the sequence and choose Batch Capture from the Bin menu. This one-click solution seems like the best answer, but it's not. The best way is to Decompose your sequence.

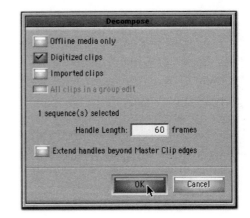

1 Put a copy of your sequence in a bin of its own.

2 If your audio does not need to be redigitized, delete the audio tracks from your copy in the Decompose bin (not the original!).

3 With the sequence selected, choose Decompose from the Clip menu.

4 In the Decompose Window, uncheck "Offline media only" and choose "Digitized clips." Handle Length indicates how much extra media the system will capture beyond what's in the sequence. This is good if you need to trim or add transitions. Click OK.

5 The Decompose process will fill your bin with a lot of clips, all labeled with the suffix ".new."

6 Now you're at the point where you have an advantage over batch-capturing the sequence, because you can sort the clips based on tape and timecode and see what tapes will be needed to do the upres as well as how many clips from each tape.

7 Select groups of clips from the same tape and go to the Batch Capture selection in the Bin menu to upres them.

8 When you're done with the video, cut the audio from the offline version back under the new video tracks.

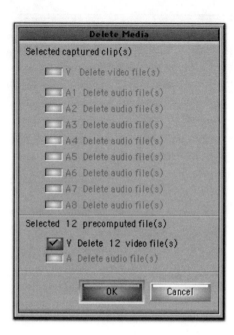

Search and Destroy Unused Media

One of the best and least painful ways to get some extra space on the drives is to delete unused precomputes, or renders. Each time you render something, even just to test the length of a dissolve, or if you had a typo in a title that has since been fixed, it stays on your drives, eating up space. Finding and deleting this media is easy. And even if you delete a render that you shouldn't have deleted, all you have to do is re-render.

❶ From the Tools menu, choose Media Tool.

❷ Choose All Drives and Current Project and Precompute Clips from the available buttons. This calls up every precompute in your project.

❸ Select any sequences in a project for which you want to save the renders.

❹ From the Bin menu, choose Select Media Relatives. This highlights all of the precomputes in the Media Tool—and any of your bins—that are "related to" those sequences.

⑤ Select the Media Tool and from the Bin menu choose Reverse Selection. This inverts all of the highlights, so that now all of the precomputes that aren't associated with your selected sequences are highlighted.

⑥ Press the Delete key. This calls up the Delete Media Window so that you can confirm the media you are about to delete. Click OK to proceed with the deletion, or you can alter your selections or cancel the operation.

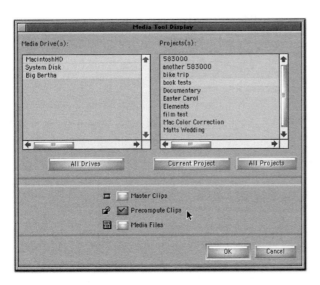

Check Media Tool on All Drives

Occasionally, it's a good idea to take a quick peek at all of the media on your drives. We've worked places where this hasn't been done in a long time, and there are parts of projects that are years old sitting on the drives.

❶ Open the Media Tool by choosing Media Tools from the Tools menu (by this time you probably should have mapped it to your keyboard).

❷ In the Media Tool choose All Drives, All Projects and select Master Clips, Precompute Clips and Media Files. Click OK.

❸ It may take a while for the Media Tool window to appear if you have a lot of media.

❹ When the Media Tool window opens, you can use the Headings selection under the Bin menu to determine headings that you want to search. For this search and destroy mission, some good headings are Creation Date (so you know how old the file is) and Project.

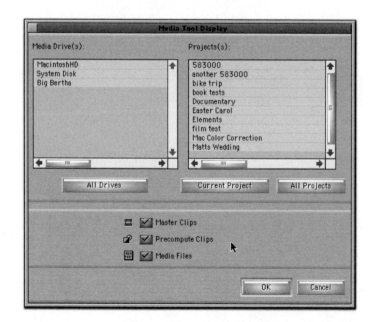

⑤ To sort the Media Tool based on the Project heading, click on the Project heading in the Media Tool window then Ctrl+E (Cmd+E).

⑥ Scroll down the list looking for odd bits and pieces from long-dead projects. Precomputes are usual culprits to be sitting around long after they've outlived their usefulness. Use basic selection methods to select multiple files and delete the ones that you no longer need. To delete all of the files from a single project it is faster to reopen the Media Tool, selecting only that project, then deleting all the files.

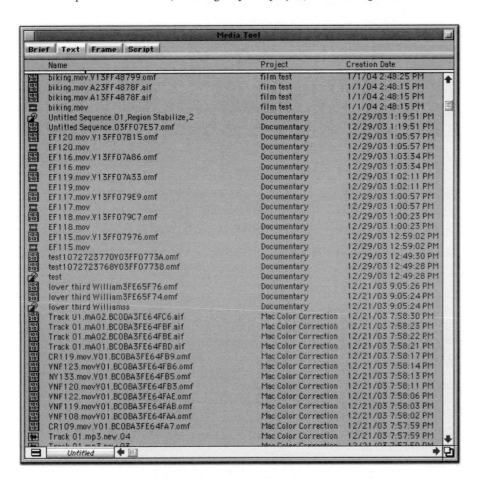

ON THE SPOT

Troubleshooting

Of course you don't ever have computer problems—but just in case, let us show you what to do when things go wrong. Step 1: Don't Panic; Step 2: Keep Reading. Seriously, there are a lot of things that can happened when you pack a computer full with tons of software, lots of specialty hardware, and an Internet connection. Things will go wrong—we know! Let us share some excellent tips with you about how to recover and move on

Where's That fnSwitch?

For all of you PowerBook and iBook users, your function keys (F1–12) may be reserved for settings such as screen brightness, volume control, and keyboard backlight. This default system behavior may interfere with any Avid commands you may want to map to these keys, because you have to hold the fn key for them to work properly. No longer, if you install a free third-party product called fnSwitch.

In Mac OS 10.3.3, this default system behavior can be inversed in the Keyboard & Mouse System Preferences so that F1–12 are always active, and you have to hold the fn key to control screen brightness, volume control, and keyboard backlight. Mac OS 10.2 users can gain this functionality by installing a free third-party preference pane called fnSwitch 1.0.1. You can find it at http://prdownloads.sourceforge.net/fnswitch/.

Command or uControl?

For new Windows-to-Mac switchers who are still stuck in the habit of pressing Ctrl instead of Cmd, there's a free third-party keyboard remapper called uControl.

http://gnufoo.org/ucontrol/

In addition to giving PowerBook and iBook users their F1–F12 keys in Mac OS 10.2, uControl can swap the Cmd and Ctrl keys, make Shift-Delete behave like a Forward Delete, and program that secondary Enter key to be another Option key.

Someone Stole My Window!

Sometimes it is possible to "lose" an important window, such as the Timeline window or the Composer window. When this happens, select the missing window from the Tools menu. Then go to the Windows menu and choose Home or press Ctrl+' (Cmd+') (apostrophe). This will call the window back into its default location.

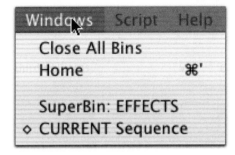

Check the Specs

Most problems with Xpress Pro are a result of having something on your system that doesn't conform with Avid's specifications. These specs change with each release, so if you're having trouble you should check the Xpress Pro specifications page on Avid's web site. This page has a list of all operating systems and hardware qualified for use with the current release of Xpress Pro and should definitely be your first stop if you're putting together a new system. You can find it at: http://www.avid.com/products/xpresspro/specs.asp.

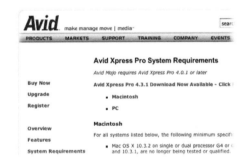

The Latest and Greatest

From time to time, Avid releases updates to Xpress Pro. These updates add new functions, fix bugs, and improve performance. Best of all, they're free to registered users. You'll find Xpress Pro updates at www.avid.com/products/xpresspro/specs.asp. While new releases fix bugs, new ones can crop up, so if you're in the middle of a project, wait until you have some downtime to install a new version–and make sure to read the release notes which contain information on known bugs and issues.

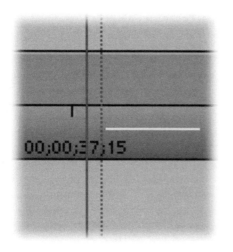

Trouble Signs

If you're experiencing playback problems, such as dropped frames or realtime effects not working, check out the Timeline performance indicators at the bottom of the timecode track. You'll see a colored line under the frames that Xpress Pro is having difficulty playing.

- A yellow line means that the processors on your system is at its limit.

- A blue line means that your drives are having trouble reading the media.

- The dreaded red line means that frames are being dropped.

You'll always see a yellow or blue line before a red line, so that will tell you the cause of the dropped frames.

Ram-a-Lam-a-Ding-Dong

RAM is like money–you can never have enough–and boy does Xpress Pro like RAM. Even though you can get by with the minimum amount required to run Xpress Pro, you'll get much better performance if you load your system with as much RAM as you can afford. Currently, Xpress Pro without Mojo requires 512MB of RAM–add the Mojo and you'll need at least 1GB. We keep at least 1GB in our systems regardless. RAM is pretty cheap these days, so go for as much as your system can handle.

Be aware that RAM which is not supported by your computer's manufacturer can caused conflicts with Xpress Pro, so check your RAM to make sure it is specifically supported by the manufacturer. Even if it's working okay for most functions, it is good to check it.

Boot It

No, we don't mean kick your computer (although we're certainly tempted to do it now and then). If things aren't running the way they should, try rebooting your system. When you're experiencing unusual behavior in Xpress Pro, sometimes all you need to do is quit the application and reset your computer. This not only goes for Xpress Pro, but other applications as well. To properly reset your computer, don't click Restart but shut it down, wait 30 seconds or so, then start 'er up again.

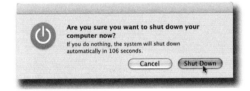

A Helping Hand

Everyone needs a helping hand now and then. When things just aren't going your way, you'll find several Internet-based Avid user forums a mouse click away.

- Creative Cow's Avid forum is frequented by many renowned experts (including the humble authors of this book). The discussion threads cover all areas of the Avid universe, and quite a bit of it is focused on Xpress Pro. Check it out at www.creativecow.net.

- DMN's Worldwide User Groups (WWUG) has a forum specifically for Xpress Pro users. It can be found at www.dmnforums.com.

- The Avid Community Forums have Xpress Pro customer support forums for both PC and Mac. Follow the Forums link from the Support menu on the Avid homepage at www.avid.com.

- The venerable Avid-L is a mailing list which is the oldest discussion forum in existence. You can sign up for it and search its archives, at http://www.avid.com/community/maillist/index.html.

Drive It Away

If Xpress Pro is having trouble playing back media, there's a good chance one of your media drives could be the culprit. If you find that media on a specific drive is problematic, then a deteriorating drive is a real possibility. Copy the media on the suspect drive to a different drive (even your system drive) and see if that fixes the problem. Once the media is on a different drive, try a low-level format on the suspect drive to block out bad sectors. Be aware that this will erase all of the data on that drive. Once that's done, copy your media back to that drive and see if things have improved. If not, it's probably time to replace that drive.

Capture Tool Held Captive

Difficulty capturing from or recording to a deck or camcorder can be caused by a faulty drive, a bad cable, a bad tape, or the device itself. If you're having trouble in this area, try the following:

- Make sure your deck is turned on.

- Select Check Decks from the pop-up menu beneath the Capture Tool Play button.

- Capture to a different drive.

- Try a different tape.

- Try another deck.

- Reload the driver for the deck.

- Connect the deck to a different FireWire port.

- Make sure all cables are properly connected.

- Try a different cable.

- Check with your drive manufacturer for any firmware updates.

Drive Before You Turn the Key

You're excited to get started, but it is important to follow directions. Don't plug in the dongle until you have installed the software and the Sentinel drivers. The Sentinel drivers tell your computer how to look at the dongle to verify it. If the drivers aren't loaded and the computer restarted, you could actually damage the dongle. By the way, replacement dongles aren't cheap.

Huh?

Avid's error messages can be rather cryptic. If Xpress Pro presents you with one and you find yourself scratching your head, try taking a look at Avid's Error Messages web page at support.avid.com/support/AvidMain.nsf/ErrorR3?ReadForm. It not only explains what many of those error codes mean, but it also gives some solutions for fixing the problem that caused the error message in the first place.

Third-Party Pooper

If you're having trouble with any of the third-party applications that come bundled with Xpress Pro, check the web site for that particular application and download any available updates or patches. This will often fix the problem.

- Boris: www.borisfx.com/download/patches.php

- ReelDVD: support.sonic.com

- Sorenson Squeeze: www.sorenson.com/support/downloads.php

- Elastic Gasket: www.profoundeffects.com/support

Even if there's no update or patch available, these web pages have support info that can help you troubleshoot.

Monitor Overlap

If you're using more than one monitor, make sure that the Composer window isn't straddling the two monitors–if it overlaps by even one pixel your video won't play back properly. You can fix this by dragging the Composer window so it doesn't straddle both your monitors. Alternately, you can click on the Composer window and select Windows>Home, or select one of the Toolsets from the Toolset menu.

Also, be aware that certain display cards will only play back video on one monitor and not the other, so if you're having playback issues try dragging the Composer window to the other monitor (while making sure it doesn't overlap).

Toolset
Basic
Color Correction
✓ Source/Record Editing
Effects Editing
Audio Editing
Capture

Save Current
Restore Current to Default
Link Current to...

Keeping Track

Xpress Pro keeps track of your media by creating media database files. Every drive on your system that has Xpress Pro media on it will has 'em. On the root level of each drive, Xpress Pro creates a folder called OMFI MediaFiles which contains the media and the databases. These databases are essential to the operation of Xpress Pro, but can become corrupt now and then, especially if you have a large amount of media. If you're getting any type of OMFI error message, trashing these database files should be one of your first steps in troubleshooting.

Repeat these steps for each of the drives on your system that contain Xpress Pro media:

❶ Quit Xpress Pro.

❷ On the root level of the drive, locate and open the folder OMFI MediaFiles.

❸ Locate the files msmMMOB.mdb and msmFMID.pmr within this folder and drag them to the Recycle Bin on a PC or the Trash on a Mac.

Once you've trashed the database files on all your media drives, launch Xpress Pro. It will scan your drives and build new database files. This might take a couple of minutes, so hang tight.

OMFI MediaFiles

Keep It Clean

Avoid cluttering your system with applications not related to your editing work. Extension and resource files from other applications can easily interfere with Xpress Pro's ability to operate properly. Do you have a problem that started after you installed some new software? If that's the case then there's a good chance that software is the cause of your woes. Uninstall it and see if the problem goes away. Running the application's uninstaller is the best way. You may need to consult the documentation or support site of the specific software to make sure you are uninstalling all the supporting files of the suspect application.

Gotta Keep 'Em Separated

Computer viruses are a fact of life, and the last thing you need is to have one of those nasty little buggers bring down your Xpress Pro system. Sure, Microsoft and Apple post updates to their OS that offer some protection against new viruses, but it's best not to install these updates until Avid qualifies them. It's a bit of a catch-22, and the best way to handle it is to keep your Xpress Pro system off the Internet entirely. It's best to have a separate machine for your office tasks like e-mail and web browsing, and keep your Xpress Pro system dedicated to editing and other creative work. If this isn't feasible, then consider creating a dual boot system with one partition for Xpress Pro and another for office stuff. You can also use a removable drive bay and keep one drive for Xpress Pro and another for everything else. That way if your system is infected with an Internet-borne virus, your Xpress Pro partition will remain unharmed.

If you decide to keep your Xpress Pro system connected to the Internet, then get your hands on the best anti-virus software you can afford and make sure to update it on a regular basis.

I've Lost My Mojo!

If you get a "Mojo no longer connected" error when launching Xpress Pro, try the following:

- Disconnect and reconnect the FireWire cable from both the Mojo and your computer.

- Power down the Mojo, wait 30 seconds, and power it up again.

- Make sure the Host light on the Mojo is on. If it isn't then try a different FireWire cable.

- Make sure there are no other devices on the FireWire bus to which Mojo is attached. Mojo sucks up all the bandwidth on the FireWire bus, and other devices, such as drives, need to be connected to a different bus, which usually means having a second FireWire card in your system.

- Disconnect the network cable from the back of your computer. The network card may share bandwidth with the FireWire port, and cause an overdraw issue.

My Mojo Has Gotten Firmer

Mojo has a Field Programmable Gate Array (FPGA), which means functionality can be added to it via a firmware update. When you install a new version of Xpress Pro, it will most likely install this sort of firmware update on your Mojo. If you're presented with a dialog asking if you want to update Mojo's firmware, select Yes. Once the firmware update is complete, make sure to quit Xpress Pro. You'll then need to cycle the power on the Mojo (turn it off, wait 30 seconds, then turn it on again). Relaunch Xpress Pro, and enjoy a better Mojo!

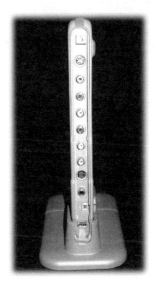

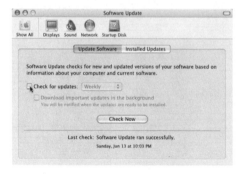

The Latest but Not the Greatest

Mac OS 10 and Windows XP have automatic update features which download and install updates to their operating systems when they become available. Unfortunately, updating your operating system can result in a system that Xpress Pro and Xpress DV will not run on. Disable the auto-updater on your system to keep this from happening, and only update your OS when you see it's been blessed on the Xpress Pro or Xpress DV Specifications webpage.

On a PC:

❶ Click the Start button and select Control Panel.

❷ Make sure the Control Panel window is in Classic View. If not, click on Switch to Classic View.

❸ Double-click the "System" Control Panel. The System Properties dialog appears.

❹ Click on the Automatic Updates tab.

❺ Click the box next to Keep my Computer up to Date so the checkmark disappears, and click OK.

On a Mac:

❶ Select Apple Menu>System Preferences.

❷ In the System Preferences dialog, click on Software Update.

❸ In the Software Update dialog, click the box to the left of Check for updates so the checkmark disappears.

Lo-Res Lowdown

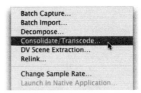

If you're trying to capture at Xpress Pro's 15:1s resolution and are getting error messages, chances are your system is having problems capturing and transcoding to 15:1s simultaneously. If you select 15:1s as your capture resolution, what Xpress Pro or Xpress DV does is capture DV25 and simultaneously transcode it to 15:1s. Slower systems are unable to do the capture and transcode all at once, so the workaround for this is to capture at DV25 and then manually transcode the media.

❶ Capture your clip(s) at DV25 resolution.

❷ Select the master clip(s) in the bin.

❸ Click on the Bin Fast Menu and select Consolidate/Transcode. The Consolidate/Transcode dialog appears

❹ In the upper-left corner of the dialog, click on the oval next to "Transcode" so it turns purple.

❺ In the Target Drive(s) area, select the drive(s) you would like your 15:1s media to be written to.

❻ From the Target Video Resolution pulldown menu, select "15:1s".

❼ Click the Transcode button.

The time it takes to transcode your media will depend on the speed of your system – on a slower machine expect it to be slower than realtime.

Gut Renovation

When all else fails, you might need to rebuild your system from the ground up. This means wiping the drives clean, reinstalling the OS and drivers, and re-installing Xpress Pro or Xpress DV (and any other software on your system). Even though this should generally be done only as a last-resort, you'll have the benefit of a brand-new "virgin" system (kind of the same feeling as driving a new car). We know a few big broadcasters and post-houses that rebuild their Avids on a monthly basis. Even though this is a bit extreme, it keeps the systems running at top-shape.

Make sure you have installer discs for your operating system, applications, and drivers (for all your hardware) before you begin this process. And, of course, make sure to back up your Projects, Users, Attic and AVX_Plugins folders.

The Hassle-Free Upgrade

It's always exciting to install a new Xpress Pro or Xpress DV upgrade. Issues can arise when you update your software, so take these precautions and you'll minimize any possible downtime:

- Never upgrade in the middle of an important project, unless you've been having trouble with your system and the upgrade is intended to fix it.

- Back up all of your projects.

- Trash your user settings. User settings can cause more problems than any other issue during an upgrade.

- On a PC, user settings can be found at C:\Program Files\Avid\Avid Xpress Pro\Avid Users.

- On a Mac, user settings can be found at Macintosh HD/Users/Shared/XpressPro.

- Disconnect your Mojo and all other FireWire devices, and re-attach them after you run the update installer and shut down.

- Check for new versions of 3rd party software, such as plug-ins, that may need to be installed.

Unplugged

AVX is Avid's plug-in architecture and everything that shows up in your effects palette is an AVX plug in (they're made by Avid and many 3rd party developers).

If you get an AVX error while launching or using Xpress Pro or Xpress DV, there might be a corrupt effect plug-in. Here's how to weed out the bad apple:

1. Quit Xpress Pro or Xpress DV.

2. On Windows navigate to C:\Program files\Avid\AVX, or on a Mac go to Macintosh HD/Applications/Avid Xpress Pro/Supporting Files/AVX.

3. Create a new folder on the your desktop called Temporary.

4. Move the contents of the AVX folder to your new Temporary folder.

5. Re-launch Xpress Pro or Xpress DV.

6. If Xpress Pro or Xpress DV launches without an AVX error, quit Xpress Pro or Xpress DV.

7. Isolate the bad plug-in by moving one of the AVX plug-ins from your Temporary folder back to the AVX folder then re-launching the Avid. If it launches without error, quit.

8. Repeat step 7 until the error message returns. Remove the plug-in that you moved last, and re-launch.

Acknowledgments

We would like to thank everyone at CMP for their patience and skill at shepherding this project to its successful completion, especially Gail Saari, Dorothy Cox, and Paul Temme. Thanks also to Jim Feeley for introducing us to the talented and dedicated publishing team at CMP.

We'd also like to thank the On the Spot editor, Rich Harrington, for his even-keeled navigation of the sometimes stormy waters of a collaborative project. You always kept your eyes on that North Star.

There is also an important "second family" that has always provided knowledge and wisdom, and that is the great team of folks up in Tewksbury (Avid Technology) who are always happy to lend a hand and provide the right tidbit of information at the crucial moment.

Equally important in providing a constant barrage of crucial information are all our many friends on the avid-L listserve. Talk about getting schooled! We'd especially like to thank (in no particular order) Wilson Chao, Terry Curren, Bob Zelin, Frank Capria, Greg Glazier, Steve Bayes, Andre Brunger, Charles Vanderpool, Dave Spraker, Jeff Kreines, Jeff Sengpiehl, Job ter Burg, Pete Bradstock, Pete Opotowsky, Tim Wilson, Michael Phillips, James Beattie, Anne-Lise Breuning, and the Creative COW Avid Forum.

Updates

Want to receive e-mail updates for *Avid Xpress Pro and DV On the Spot*? Send a blank e-mail to avidots@news.cmpbooks.com We will do our best to keep you informed of software updates and enhancements, new tips, and other Avid Xpress resources.

Avid Xpress Pro Editing Workshop

Steve Hullfish & Jaime Fowler

Master the craft of editing with tutorial lessons that demonstrate the edit of an entire sequence with increasingly sophisticated editing techniques. Lessons cover the gamut from proper installation to sound editing, special effects, titling, and output. The companion DVD contains tutorial media and plug-ins.

$49.95, Softcover with DVD, 352 pp, ISBN 1-57820-238-8

Color Correction for Digital Video

Steve Hullfish and Jamie Fowler

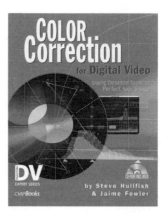

Use desktop tools to improve your storytelling, deliver critical cues, and add impact to your video. Beginning with a clear, concise description of color and perception theory, this full-color book shows you how to analyze color-correction problems and solve them—whatever NLE or plug-in you use. Refine your skills with tutorials that include secondary and spot corrections and stylized looks. The companion CD contains tutorial media and plug-ins.

$49.95, 4-color, Softcover with CD-ROM, 202 pp, ISBN 1-57820-201-9

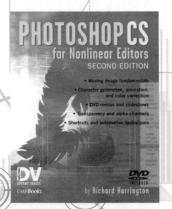

Photoshop CS for Nonlinear Editors
2nd Edtion

Richard Harrington

Use Photoshop CS to generate characters, correct colors, and animate graphics for digital video. You'll grasp the fundamental concepts and master the complete range of Photoshop tools through lively discourse, full-color presentations, and hands-on tutorials. The companion DVD contains 120 minutes of video lessons, tutorial media, and plug-ins.

$54.95, 4-color, Softcover with DVD, 336 pp, ISBN 1-57820-237-X